BRUEGEL'S
THREE SOLDIERS

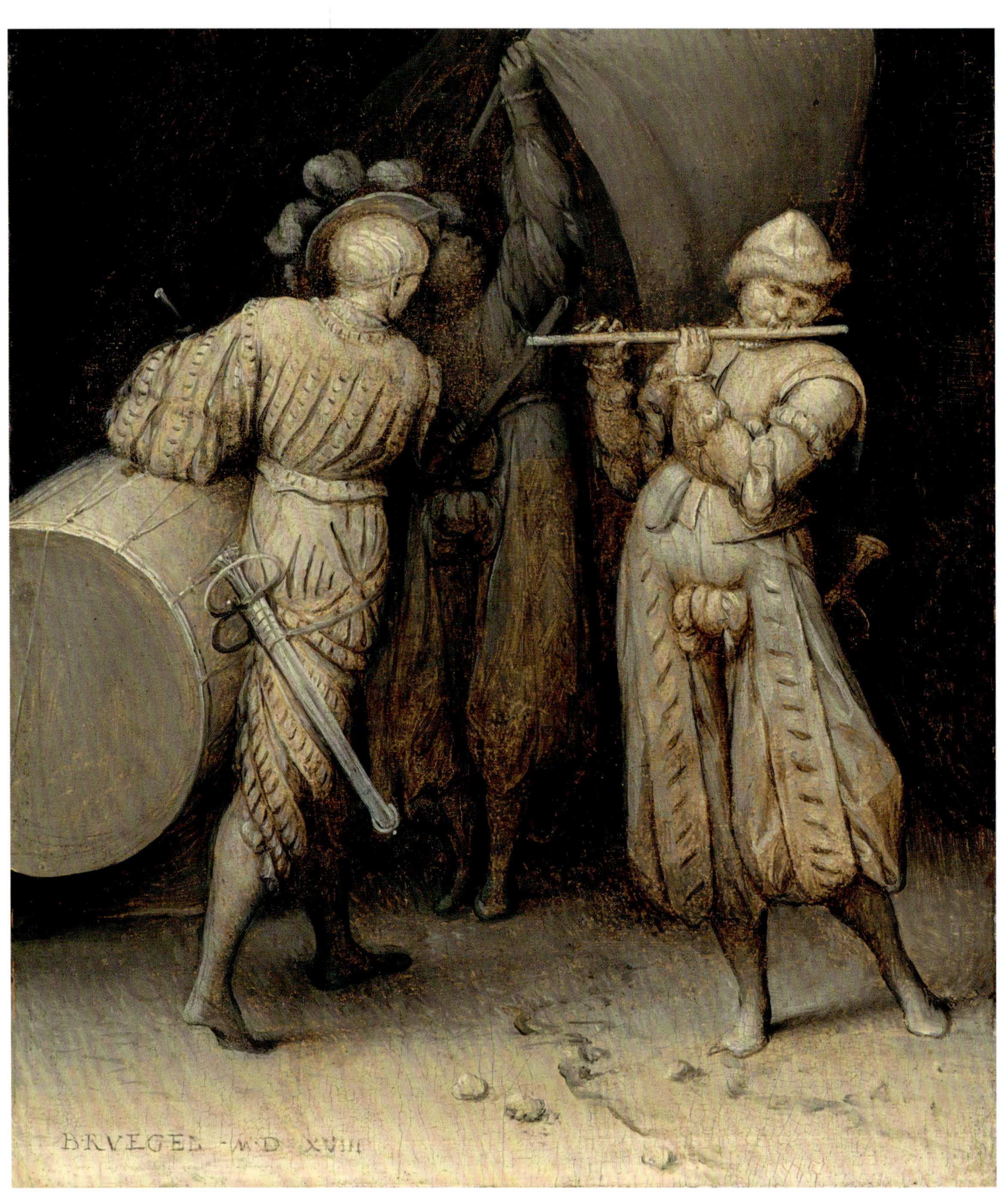

BRUEGEL'S THREE SOLDIERS

Anna-Claire Stinebring

Salman Toor

The Frick Collection, New York
in association with D Giles Limited

FRICK DIPTYCH SERIES

Designed to foster critical engagement and interest specialist and non-specialist alike, each book in this series illuminates a single work in the Frick's rich collection with an essay by a Frick curator paired with a contribution from a contemporary artist or writer.

First published in 2024 by The Frick Collection
1 East 70th Street
New York, NY 10021
www.frick.org

Michaelyn Mitchell, Editor in Chief
Gemma McElroy, Assistant Editor

In association with GILES
An imprint of D Giles Limited
66 High Street
Lewes, BN7 1XG, UK
gilesltd.com

Copyedited and proofread by Sarah Kane
Designed by Caroline and Roger Hillier,
The Old Chapel Graphic Design

Produced by GILES

Printed and bound in China

A CIP catalogue record for this book is available from the Library of Congress.

ISBN 978-1-913875-53-4

Cover and pages 6, 12: details from Pieter Bruegel the Elder, *The Three Soldiers*, 1568 (frontispiece)

Frontispiece: Pieter Bruegel the Elder, *The Three Soldiers*, 1568. Oil on panel, 8 × 7 in. (20.3 × 17.8 cm). The Frick Collection, New York; Purchased by The Frick Collection, 1965 (1965.1.163)

CONTENTS

Anna-Claire Stinebring

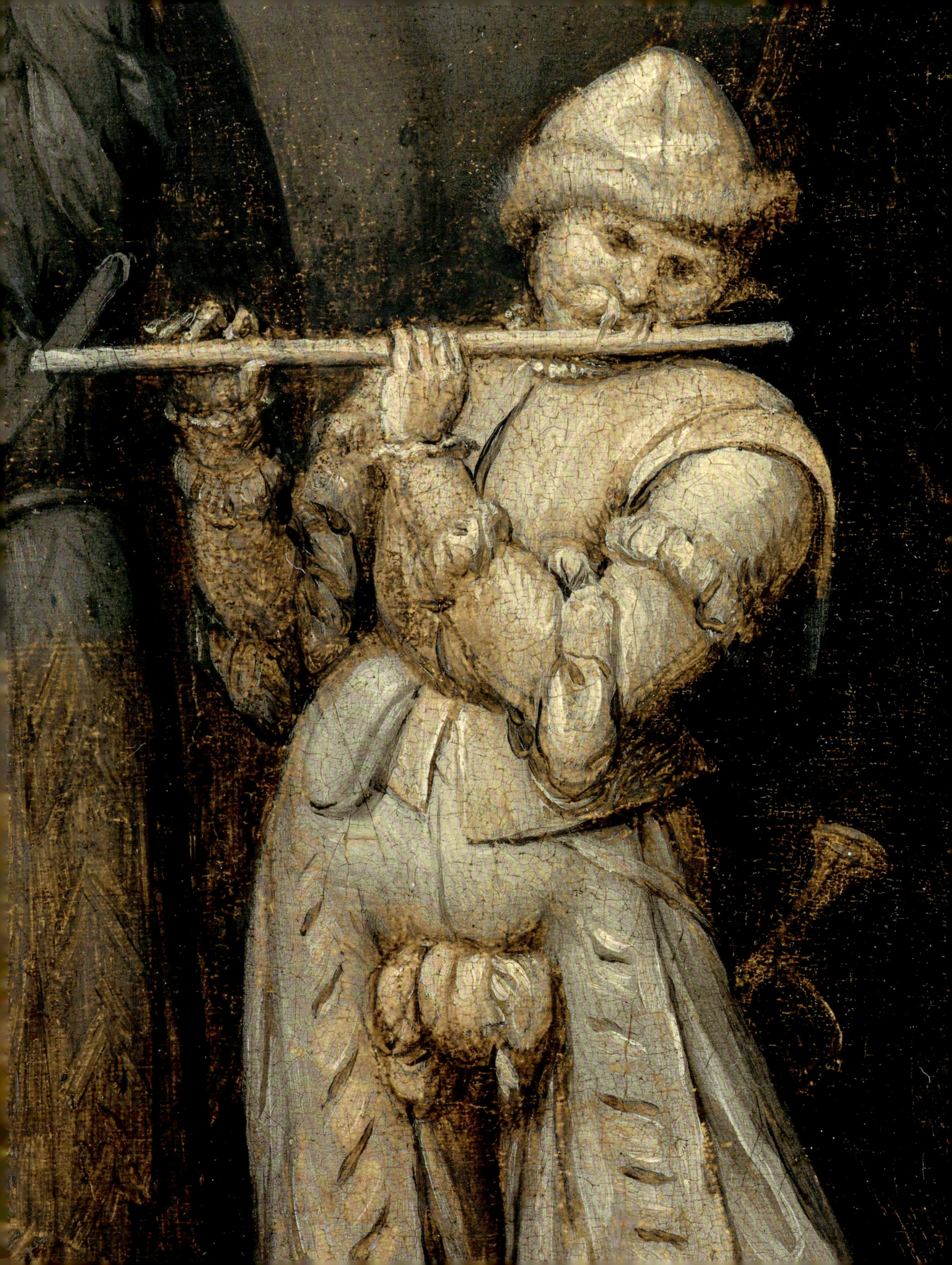

As his only known grisaille (shades of gray) painting with a secular subject, *The Three Soldiers* holds a unique place in Pieter Bruegel the Elder's oeuvre. Painted the year before his death, this delicate work depicts three stylish German mercenary foot soldiers: a standard-bearer, a flute player, and a drummer in dancer-like poses. The role of such soldiers—who were often depicted, especially in prints—was to rally the troops and lead them into battle. Once part of the illustrious collection of King Charles I of England, this refined painting is one of only three signed works by Bruegel in public collections in the United States.

In this fourteenth volume of the Frick's Diptych series, Anna-Claire Stinebring, the Frick's 2022–24 Anne L. Poulet Curatorial Fellow, investigates the historical context of *The Three Soldiers*, as well as its symbolic elements. Anna-Claire's illuminating essay is preceded by Salman Toor's inventive response to the painting, a playful portrayal of soldiers of another kind—one holding a flag, one playing a tambourine, and a third waving a banner. To both contributors we owe our sincere thanks.

At the Frick, thanks are due to Xavier F. Salomon, Deputy Director and Peter Jay Sharp Chief Curator, and to Curator Aimee Ng. Thanks also to Editor in Chief Michaelyn Mitchell, who managed the production of the publication and, with Assistant Editor Gemma McElroy, edited the text. We would also like to express our gratitude to our publishing partner D Giles Limited.

Ian Wardropper
Anna-Maria and Stephen Kellen Director, The Frick Collection

ACKNOWLEDGMENTS

First and foremost, I would like to thank Curator Aimee Ng and Xavier F. Salomon, Deputy Director and Peter Jay Sharp Chief Curator, for their exemplary mentorship during my time as a Poulet Curatorial Fellow at the Frick. This book has been enriched by their feedback and inspired by their pathbreaking curatorial work—including *Living Histories: Queer Views and Old Masters*—and would not have been possible without their vision and support. It has been a pleasure and a privilege to collaborate with Salman Toor, whose art has offered me new perspectives on monochrome painting, on artistic portrayals of male beauty, and on the often unacknowledged homosocial dimensions of quotidian aspects of society. Studying *The Three Soldiers* together in person helped me see the painting anew.

I spent a wonderful morning in front of *The Three Soldiers* with Sophie Scully, Associate Conservator at the Metropolitan Museum of Art, and my analysis of materials and technique are informed by her insights. At the Courtauld Gallery, I studied *Christ and the Woman Taken in Adultery* (unframed) with Chief Conservator Graeme Barraclough and Senior Curator of Paintings Karen Serres, whose 2016 catalogue *Bruegel in Black and White* remains indispensable. At Upton House, Property Curator Michelle Leake allowed me to study the *Death of the Virgin* on a day the house was closed. At the Museum Boijmans Van Beuningen, I had the rare opportunity to examine Bruegel's *Resurrection* drawing, with special thanks to Curator of Prints Mireille Linck. Colleagues at the Rijksmuseum, especially Leon Vosters, made possible the viewing of relevant prints.

At the Frick, my sincere thanks to Editor in Chief Michaelyn Mitchell and Assistant Editor Gemma McElroy for their expert editing, which has greatly enhanced my essay. My thanks also go to Archive Lead Susan Chore and others at the Frick Art Reference Library, especially Reference Lead Joey Vincennie. Conversations with Giulio Dalvit, Assistant Curator of Sculpture, about the sculptor Jacques Jonghelinck, indirectly informed my research.

Giulio and Marie-Laure Buku Pongo, Assistant Curator of Decorative Arts, both of whom have authored books in the Frick's Diptych series, offered insights about the Diptych essay structure. Conservation Assistant Regan Martin helped with conservation documentation, and Patrick King, Head of Art Preparation and Installation, and Christopher Roberson, Preparator, made possible examination of the painting unframed.

Larry Silver, James and Nan Wagner Farquhar Professor Emeritus of History of Art at the University of Pennsylvania, first suggested *The Three Soldiers* to me as a topic of study in 2018, and he shared his own insights on Bruegel. Maryan Ainsworth, Álvaro Saieh Curator Emerita of European Paintings at the Metropolitan Museum, invited me to speak to her graduate class at the Institute of Fine Arts about *The Three Soldiers*, on a day when Metropolitan Museum Conservator Shawn Digney-Peer also studied the painting. I likewise benefitted from a presentation I made to the Dutch and Flemish Art Working Group at the Metropolitan Museum and am grateful to Met curators Adam Eaker and Joanna Sheers Seidenstein for this opportunity. Adam generously read a draft of my essay, offering excellent feedback. Ian Wardropper, Anna-Maria and Stephen Kellen Director of the Frick, kindly introduced me to Toby Ferris's *Short Life in a Strange World: Birth to Death in 42 Panels.* For generative conversations that encouraged elements of the essay, thanks go to Emma Capron, Caitlin Henningsen, Christopher Snow Hopkins, Sarah Mallory, Jun Nakamura, and David Pullins.

As always, the enthusiasm and support of my family have been integral. This book is dedicated to my husband Adam Popp—thank you for being my art travel companion, first reader, and partner in life.

Anna-Claire Stinebring
Assistant Curator of European Paintings, The Metropolitan Museum of Art
2022–24 Anne L. Poulet Curatorial Fellow, The Frick Collection

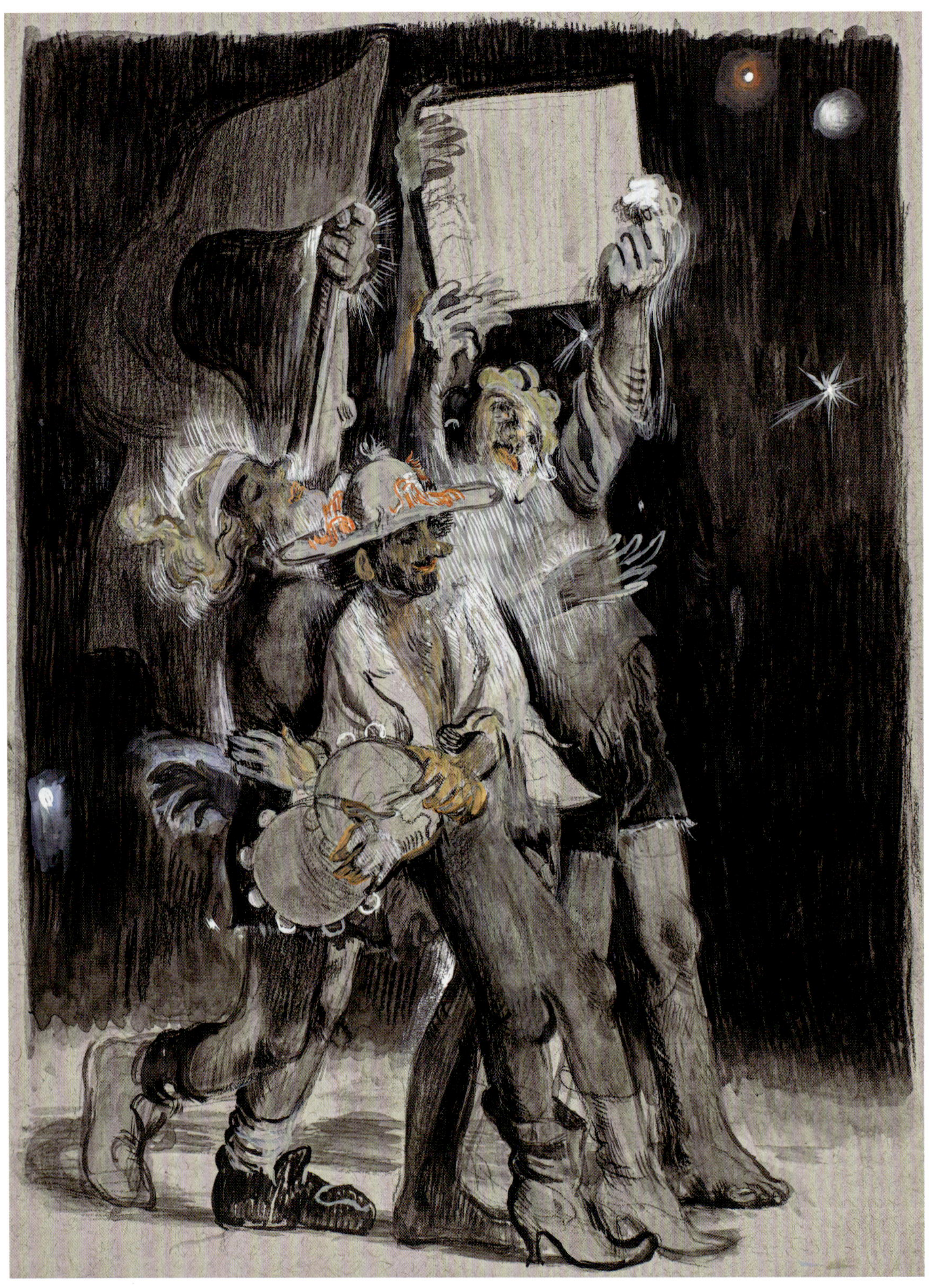

SALMAN TOOR'S
THREE MASCOTS

Salman Toor made *Three Mascots* in response to Pieter Bruegel the Elder's *Three Soldiers* of 1568. Though separated by more than four centuries, the two works and the two artists are nonetheless in conversation, allowing us to appreciate the jauntiness of Toor's mascots as compared to the elegance of Bruegel's military figures—and the manner in which each artist has, in his own way, so adeptly created such a strong sense of relationship among their figures in compositions that are at once monochromatic and rich.

Salman Toor
Three Mascots, 2023
Charcoal and gouache on paper
12 × 9 in. (30.5 × 22.9 cm)
Private collection

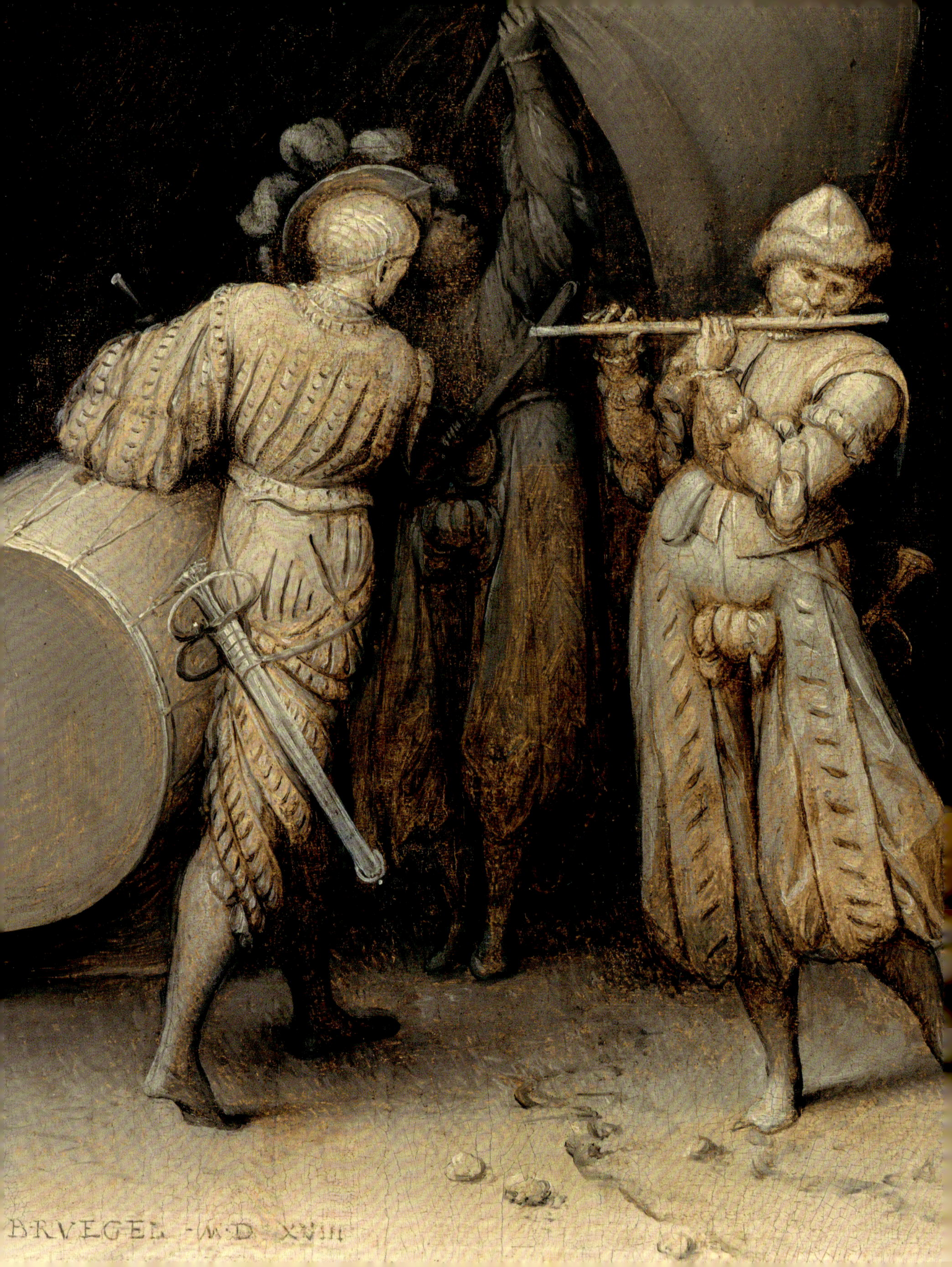
BRVEGEL · M·D· XVIII

BRUEGEL'S *THREE SOLDIERS*

Anna-Claire Stinebring

Standing in front of Pieter Bruegel the Elder's (ca. 1525–1569) *Three Soldiers* (frontispiece), visitors to The Frick Collection encounter an oak panel smaller than an 8½-by-11-inch sheet of paper. It is an oil painting in grisaille, or shades of gray. Fluid brushstrokes form a pebble-strewn ground and three men in distinctive costumes. Illuminated at left is a drummer. At right, also brightly lit, is a flute player, or fifer. Behind them, obscured by shadows, is a standard-bearer, hoisting a giant flag aloft. At lower left, the Netherlandish painter has signed the panel in a Latinized script with the date 1568 in Roman numerals (fig. 1): BRVEGEL . M. D. [L]XVIII.[1]

There is a lyricism to the scene. The men are lithe, with limbs outstretched. They maintain a lively energy despite their isolated environment. While the space may be nearly empty, it is full of sound—the music of the fife and drum and the billowing of the standard. Who are these men? Why do they appear in an undifferentiated space, drained of color? What could be the original meaning of this subdued yet captivating work, and what has been its history through the years?

As the title indicates, the men are soldiers. More specifically, they are German mercenary foot soldiers, or *Landsknechte*, identifiable by their slashed sleeves and trousers and their sturdy swords, called *Katzbalger*. In sixteenth-century

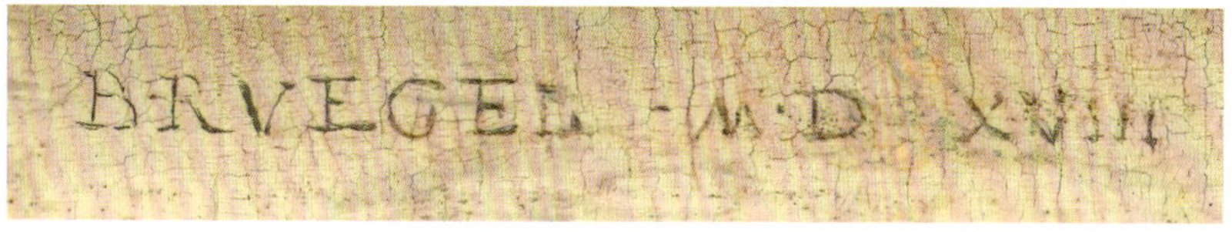

Fig. 1
Detail of Pieter Bruegel the Elder, *The Three Soldiers*, 1568 (frontispiece)

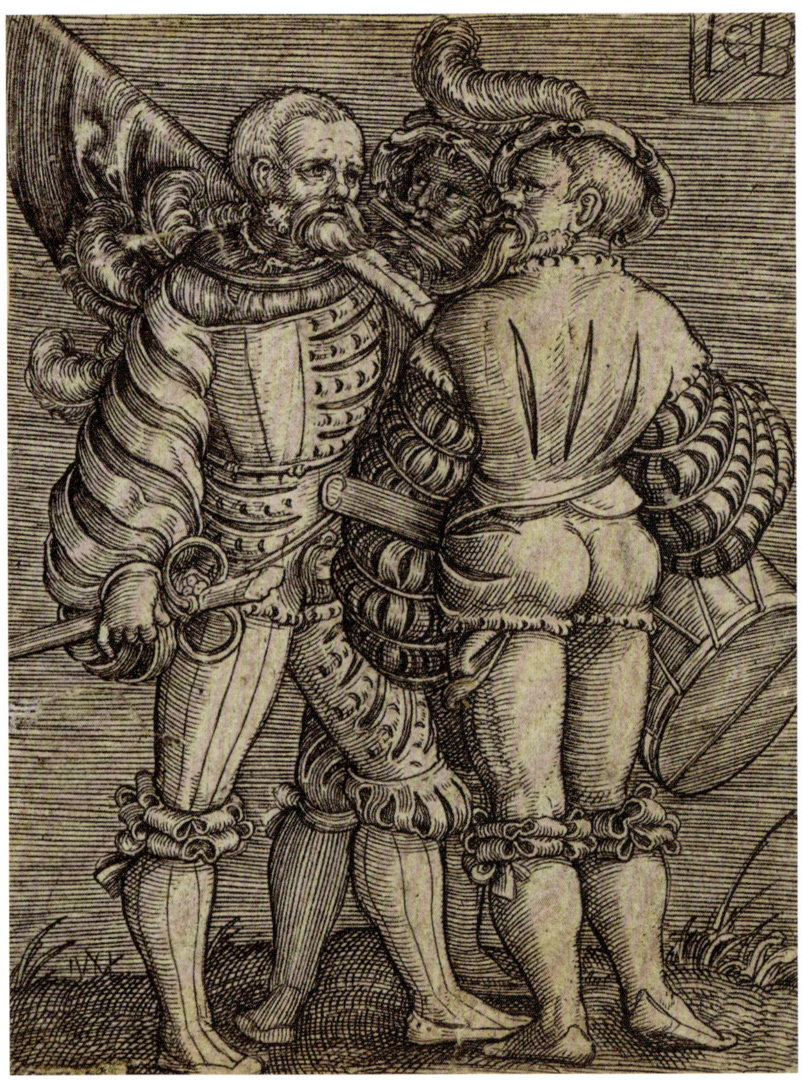

Fig. 2
Jacob Binck
*Standard-Bearer, Fifer, and
Drummer*, ca. 1550
Engraving
2¼ × 1¾ in. (5.8 × 4.5 cm)
British Museum, London

Fig. 3
Erhard Schön, with text by
Hans Sachs
Gall von Unterwalden, from the
Landsknechte series, ca. 1530
Hand-colored woodcut
11¹⁵⁄₁₆ × 7½ in. (30.3 × 19.1 cm)
Museum Boijmans Van
Beuningen, Rotterdam

northern European art, imagery of *Landsknechte* could serve a range of functions, from patriotic to critical to comedic. The grouping of standard-bearer, fifer, and drummer appears time and again, especially in prints (fig. 2). The trio's role was to rally troops and lead them into battle.

What is particularly striking about the use of grisaille in *The Three Soldiers* is that Bruegel has suppressed not only the inherent colorfulness of oil paint as a medium but also that of the costumes. In contrast, blues, reds, and yellows parade across a hand-colored series of woodcut prints of mercenaries, created

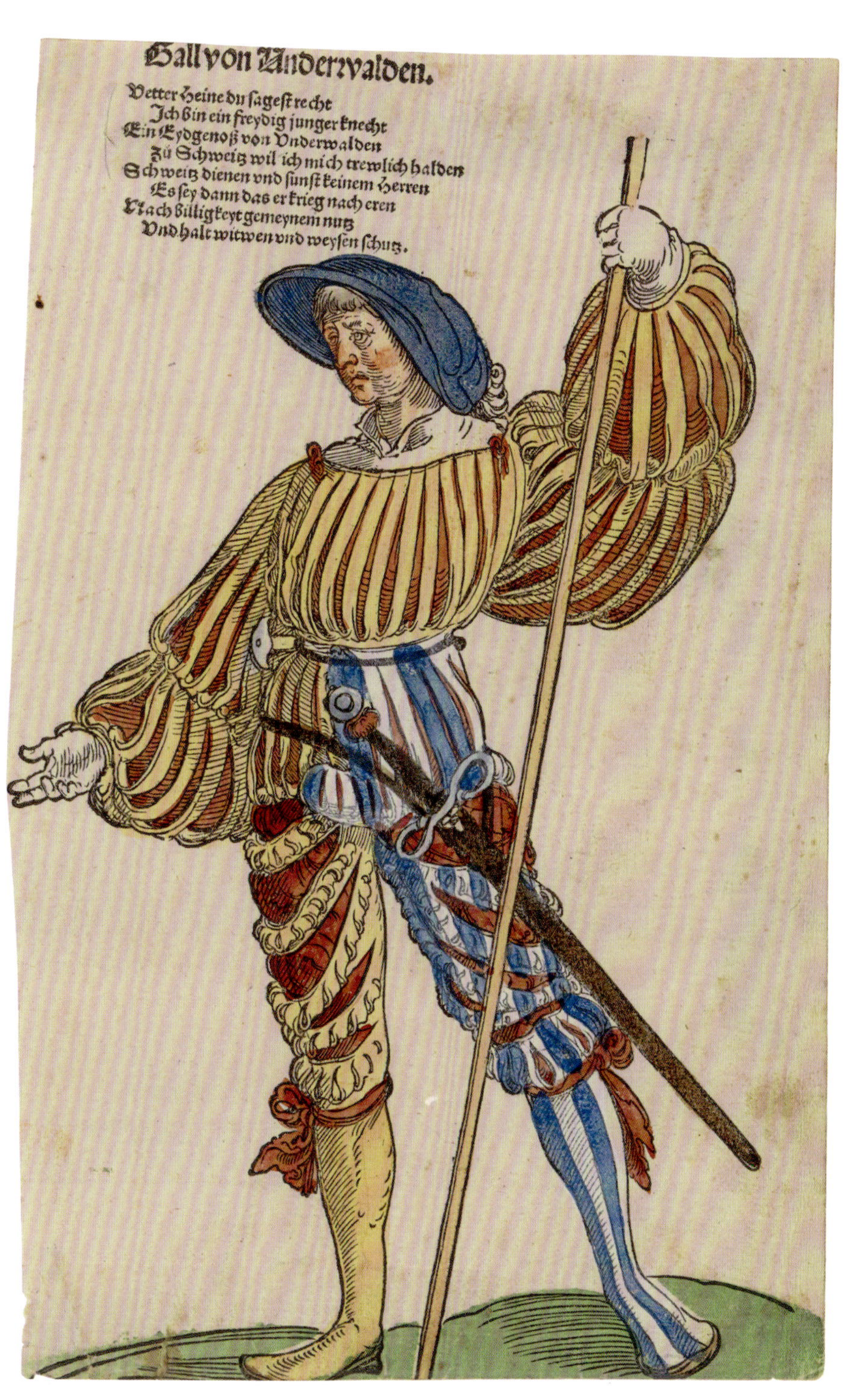

Gall von Underwalden.
Vetter Heine du sagest recht
Ich bin ein freydig junger knecht
Ein Eydgenoß von Underwalden
Zü Schweitz wil ich mich trewlich halden
Schweitz dienen vnd sunst keinem herren
Es sey dann das er krieg nach eren
Nach billigkeyt gemeynem nutz
Vnd halt witwen vnd weysen schutz.

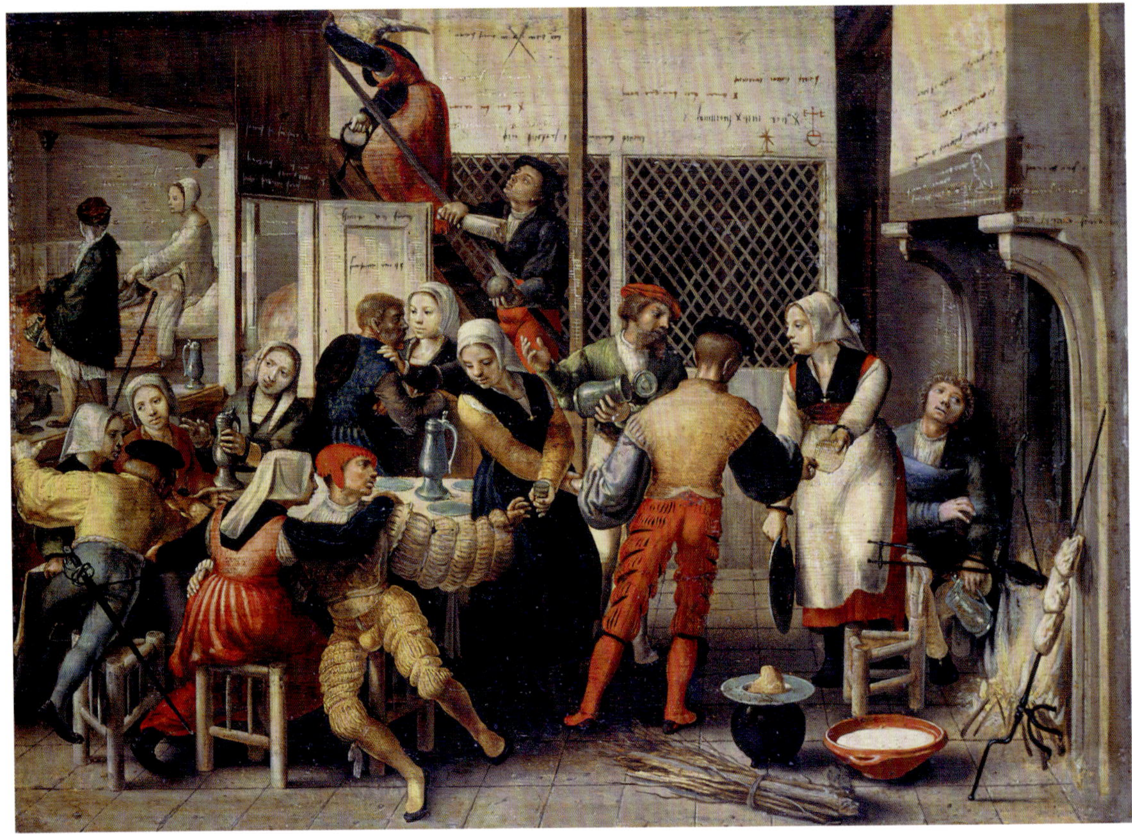

Fig. 4
Brunswick Monogrammist
Brothel Scene with Soldiers and Waffle Making, ca. 1530
Oil on panel
12⅞ × 17¹⁵⁄₁₆ in.
(32.7 × 45.5 cm)
Städel Museum, Frankfurt
am Main

Fig. 5
Lucas van Leyden
Standard-Bearer, ca. 1510
Engraving
4¹¹⁄₁₆ × 2¹³⁄₁₆ in. (11.9 × 7.1 cm)
The Metropolitan Museum
of Art, New York; The Elisha
Whittelsey Collection, The Elisha
Whittelsey Fund, 1993

in Nuremberg earlier in the century (fig. 3). Soldiers' slashed trousers of red and yellow stand out in the center foreground of a work from the 1530s by the painter known as the Brunswick Monogrammist (act. ca. 1525–ca. 1555) (fig. 4), who was active in Antwerp, where Bruegel was primarily based.[2] Certainly, many sixteenth-century prints of soldiers—such as an engraving of a standard-bearer by the Northern Netherlandish artist Lucas van Leyden (ca. 1494–1533) (fig. 5)—necessarily lack color. The suppression of color in *The Three Soldiers* is more pronounced, however, because color is inherent to the properties of oil painting, unlike engraving. Bruegel's *Three Soldiers* therefore slyly withholds visual expectations for both his chosen medium and his chosen subject.

Even in recent, illuminating studies of Bruegel's grisaille paintings, there has been no sustained exploration of how the monochrome palette and soldier imagery interact.[3] It is worth investigating further how a colorful subject—a

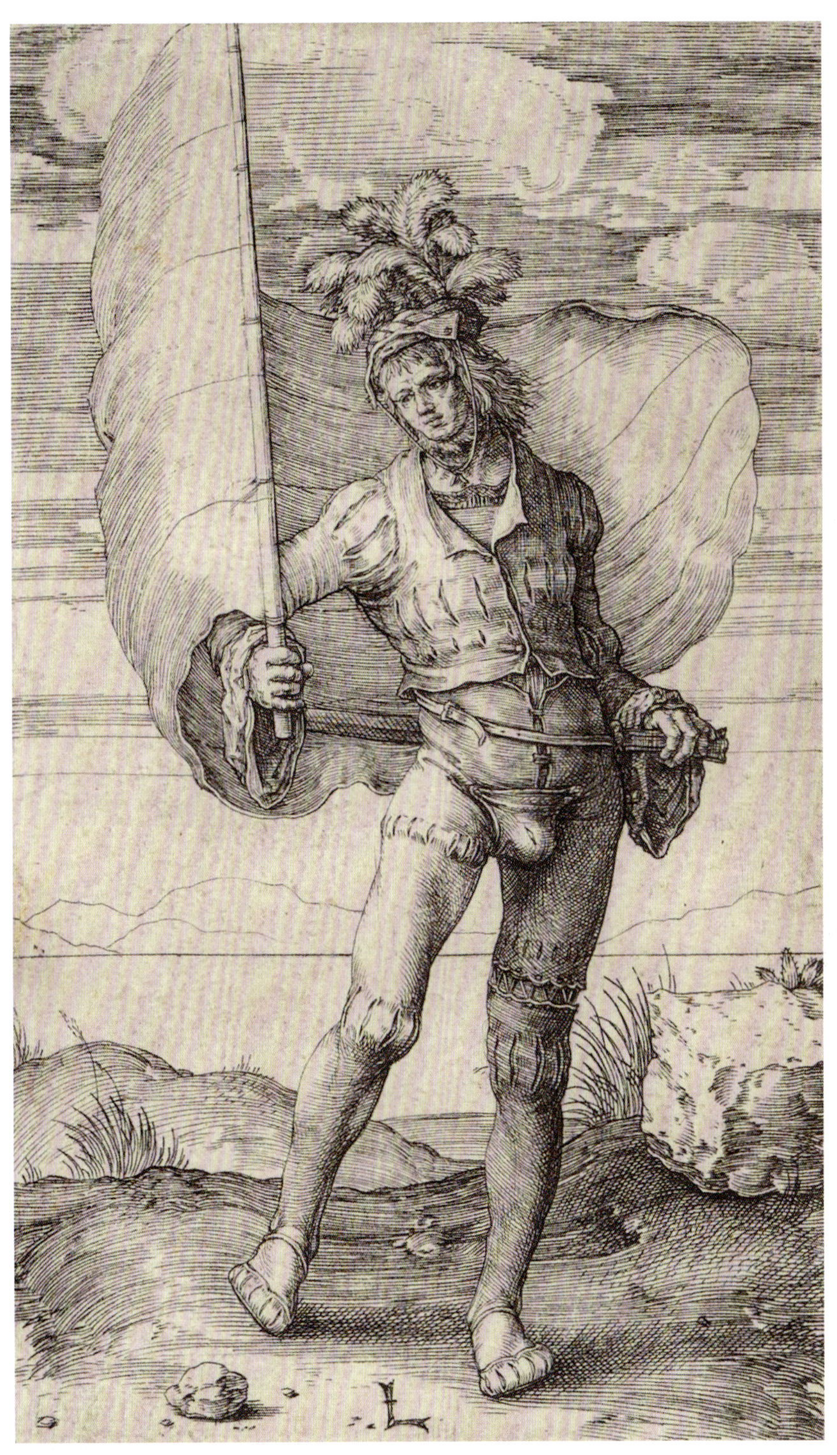

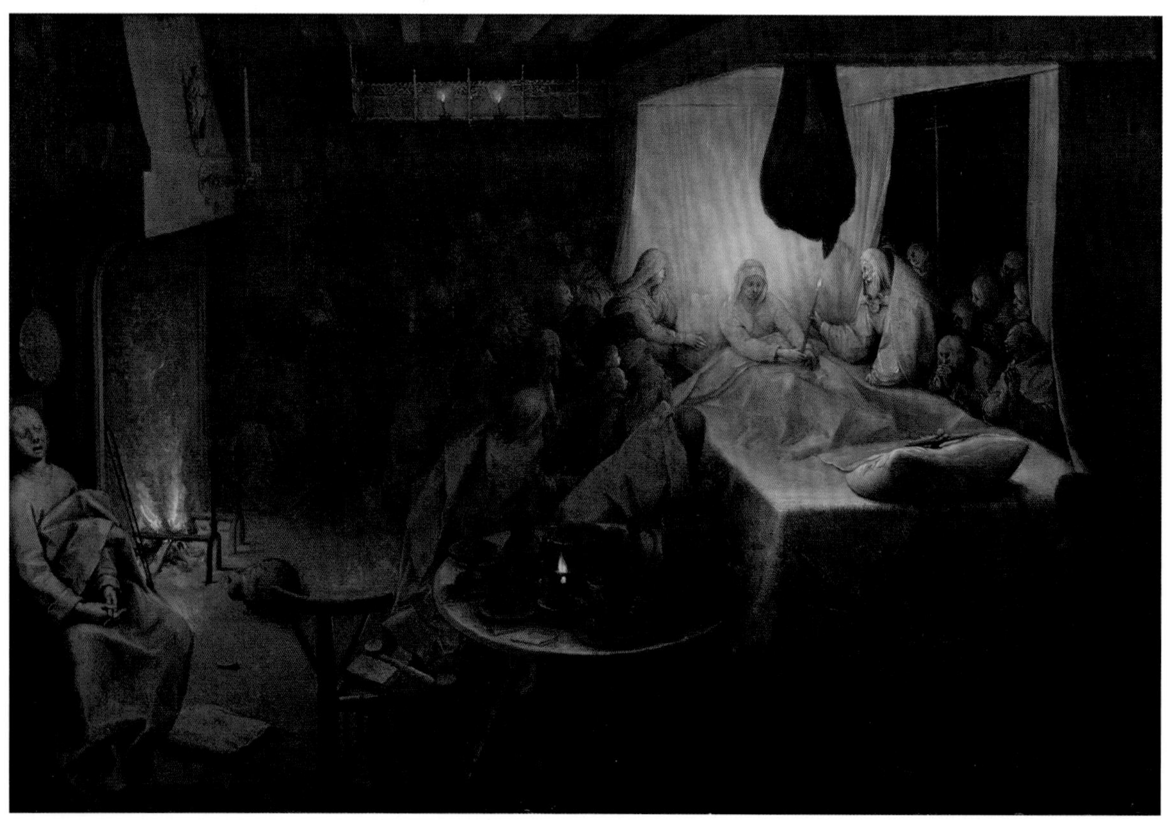

Fig. 6
Pieter Bruegel the Elder
Death of the Virgin, ca. 1562–65
Oil on panel, 14½ × 21⅞ in. (36.9 × 55.5 cm)
National Trust, Upton House, The Bearsted Collection,
Banbury, UK

subject that is, as will become clear, colorful in more than one sense of the word, through the inclusion of suggestive details—is transformed by its translation into shades of gray. This essay explores this fundamental question, closely considering the original artistic and political environment. The delicate painting whose elegant military figures seem insulated from the grim realities of war has, in fact, survived several periods of cataclysmic upheaval, both in the year it was made and in the seventeenth century. Nevertheless, first and foremost it remains playful in its details, inviting viewers to lean in, with pleasure.

A Closer Look at Bruegel's Grisailles

The Three Soldiers is one of only three extant grisaille paintings by the artist and the only one of a non-religious subject. The other two, also made in the last decade of Bruegel's career, are the *Death of the Virgin* (fig. 6) and *Christ and the Woman Taken in Adultery* (fig. 7). The three works strongly correspond in

Fig. 7
Pieter Bruegel the Elder
Christ and the Woman Taken in Adultery, 1565
Oil on panel
9½ × 13⁹⁄₁₆ in. (24.1 × 34.4 cm)
Courtauld Gallery, London
(Samuel Courtauld Trust); Count
Antoine Seilern, bequest, 1978

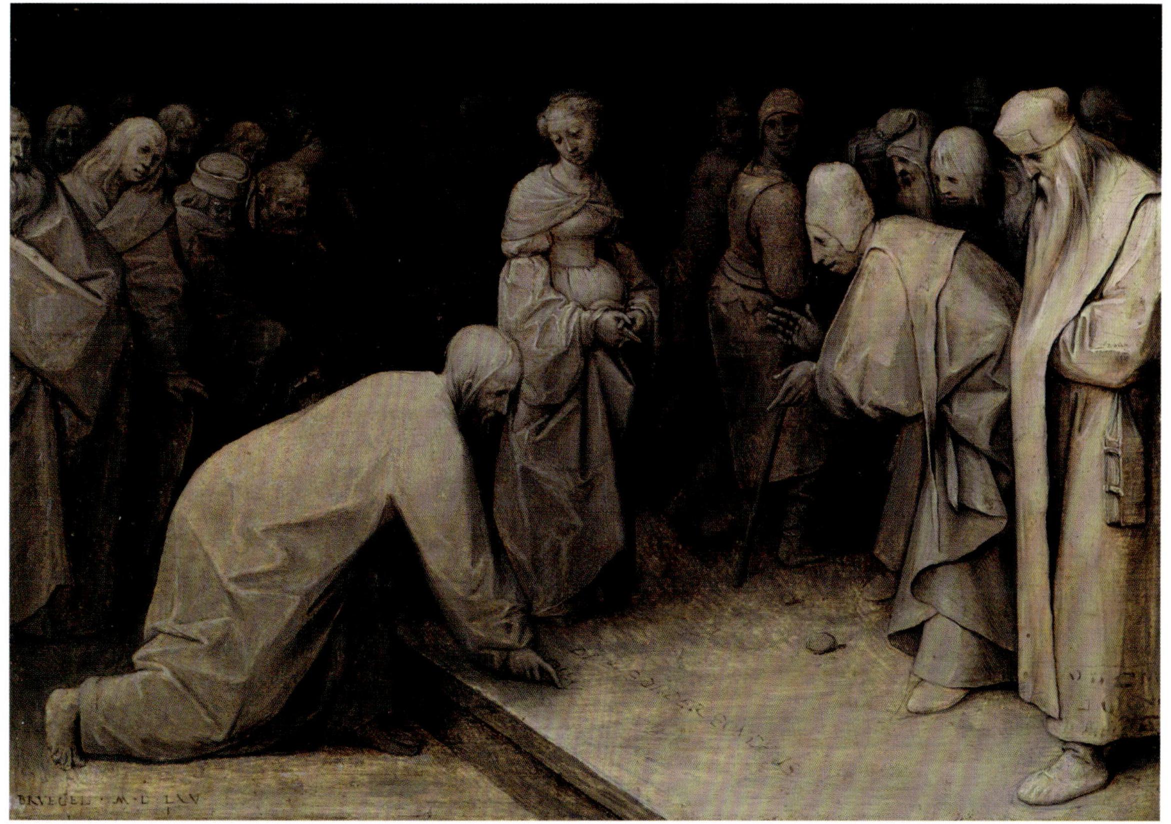

Fig. 8
IRR of Bruegel the Elder,
The Three Soldiers, 1568
(frontispiece), with arrows
indicating the underdrawn
contour of the drum. The
Metropolitan Museum of Art,
New York; Department of
Paintings Conservation

scale and technique and in their exceptional quality. They were all conceived as stand-alone works rather than preparatory studies for prints.[4]

Each grisaille is painted on a single oak panel, and each retains its original small-scale dimensions. As was standard practice at the time, the panels were first covered with a preparatory white ground layer, on which Bruegel sketched his designs in a dry medium (charcoal or chalk). In each case, Bruegel's underdrawing is minimal yet dynamic. Infrared reflectography (IRR), an imaging technique used to map the loose underdrawing in *The Three Soldiers*, shows that the final painting differs from the underdrawing in only a few places, for instance, in the barrel of the drum, which is wider than in the initial drawing (fig. 8).[5]

While Bruegel primarily mixed white and black for the gray tones, he selectively added tiny amounts of browns and reds or blues to imbue the three scenes with subtle warmth or coolness, respectively. In *The Three Soldiers*, there may be brown earth pigments mixed into the shadows.[6] However, the lighter brown glow that permeates the illuminated areas has over time become more pronounced. This is attributable at least in part to the discoloration of the current varnish and also of the white ground, which now shows through somewhat in the thinner passages of paint, due to the increased translucency of the aged oil paint and some minor wear. All three paintings would have been cooler in tone originally.[7]

Above all, the paintings share an assured and streamlined handling of paint. Bruegel worked from dark to light, starting with the black background. For *The Three Soldiers*, he left the drummer and fifer in reserve, meaning he refrained from covering the areas destined for those figures with the darker pigment. Keeping the paint thin, Bruegel utilized the white ground layer for the illuminated foreground. He only applied thicker brushstrokes of lead white for the brightest highlights, such as the drummer's sword hilt (fig. 9). Not waiting for paint to dry, Bruegel worked swiftly, in a technique termed wet-in-wet. A particularly winning detail of this technique is the mustache of the fifer (fig. 10), where Bruegel created a feathery effect and appearance of movement by dragging the loaded brush through the still-wet paint of the flute.[8]

Bruegel imbues the three soldiers with dynamism and achieves depth of space through remarkably efficient means. This is especially impressive given how easy it is for working in gradations of black and white paint, particularly when painting quickly, to devolve into a muddy mess—an undifferentiated

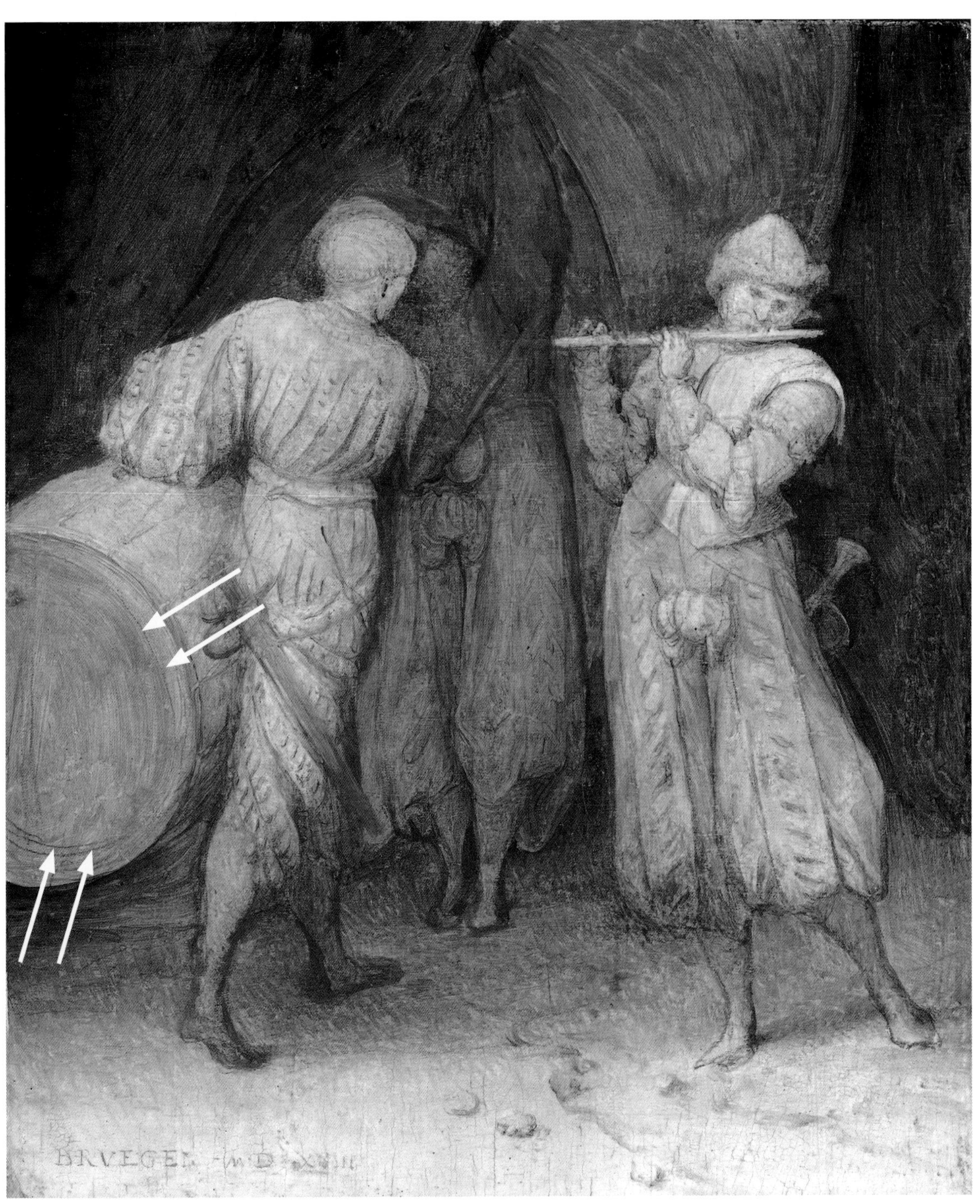

BRVEGEL MD XVII

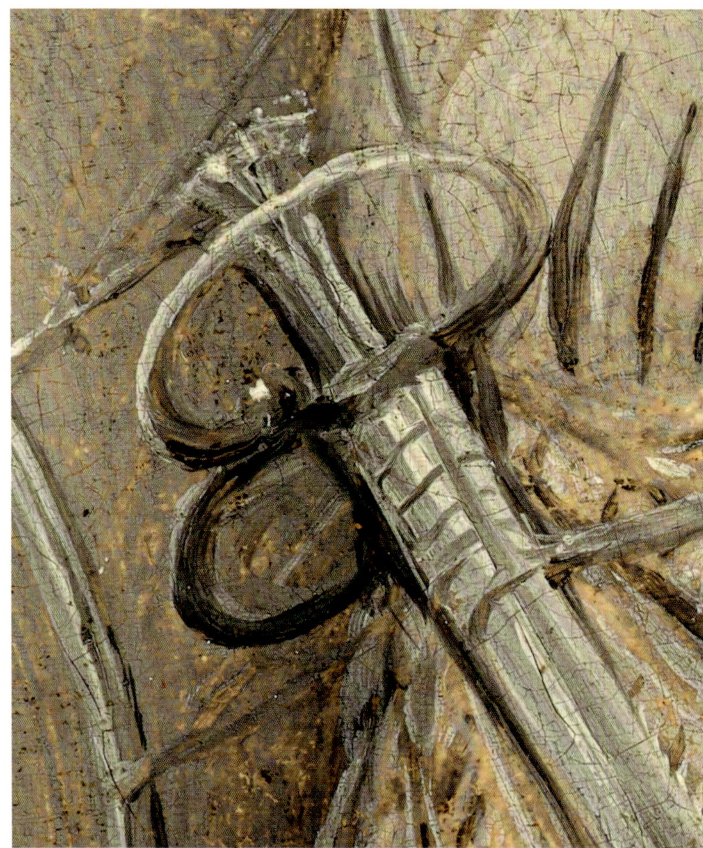

Fig. 9
Detail of Bruegel the Elder, *The Three Soldiers*, 1568 (frontispiece)

Fig. 10
Detail of Bruegel the Elder, *The Three Soldiers*, 1568 (frontispiece)

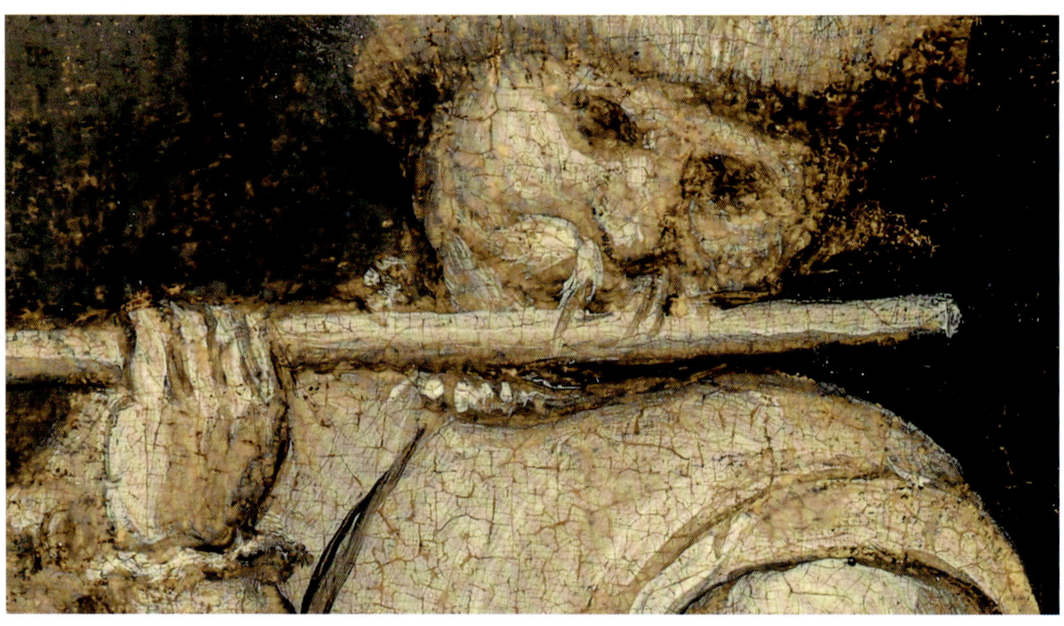

middle gray tone.[9] Creating space in grisaille is more difficult because the painter cannot fall back on contrasting colors to delineate forms. In *The Three Soldiers*, the two men in front emerge from the dark background with crispness and clarity, while the standard-bearer recedes into the rich shadows.[10]

The Grisaille Tradition: Local and Foreign Sources

In Bruegel's day, the term *grisaille* was not used to refer to works of art in shades of gray. Instead, sixteenth- and seventeenth-century inventories in Dutch describe paintings in *wit ende swert* (white and black).[11] Other commonly found terms are paintings in *gedootverft* (dead coloring) and *color lapidum* (Latin for "the color of stone"), the latter of which is an erudite term, with an ancient provenance going back to the Roman writer Pliny the Elder (23–79 CE).[12]

Color lapidum is apt for oil paintings by earlier Netherlandish masters such as Jan van Eyck (1395–1441). Working in the first half of the fifteenth century, Van Eyck used the naturalistic capabilities of the oil medium to imitate unpainted stone sculptures in exacting detail, especially on the outer wings of altarpieces. Van Eyck took care to simulate specific types of stone, from veined limestone to polished black marble, even making visual jokes that seem to assert painting's primacy. In one instance, a faux alabaster statuette of the Virgin Annunciate includes a "carved" Dove of the Holy Spirit that levitates above the Virgin, unencumbered by the supporting struts a real carving would require.[13] To fully appreciate the wit of these grisaille paintings, it is important to grasp how bright pigments, suspended in glazes, were integral to Van Eyck's uncanny ability to counterfeit details from the natural world, such as gems.[14] Oil painting in the Netherlandish tradition is distinguished by luminous color, making the choice of grisaille all the more bold.

Monochrome for the painted outer wings of altarpieces also served a devotional function. Altarpieces remained closed except on Sundays and religious feast days. A subdued aesthetic on the outer wings enhanced the splendor of the polychromed interiors when revealed.[15] Painting in grisaille was also a means of demonstrating painterly skill, following classical models. Pliny extolled Greek painters who achieved sophisticated compositions using only a limited color palette.[16] This antique tradition was well known in learned artistic circles by Bruegel's day.[17]

The phenomenon that began with Van Eyck of oil painting evoking sculpture has been characterized by scholars as the Netherlandish response to the Italian tradition of the *paragone*, or contest between the two media, which is steeped in classical sources such as Pliny. While the Italian context of the *paragone* is documented, no equivalent written evidence of such a debate exists for the Low Countries.[18] However, this does not invalidate the clear dialogue (or even competition) with sculpture visible in paintings by Van Eyck. The grisaille tradition with which Bruegel engaged—transmitted via images rather than texts—had deep local roots.

This local tradition of "black and white" painting was one of great variety, including, on the one hand, works that carried forward Van Eyck's legacy of painting sculpture and, on the other hand, works that eschewed color but did not directly imitate sculpture.[19] Sculpture was not the only medium with which painting in shades of gray was associated. The origins of grisaille in northern Europe can also be located in manuscript illumination. When Bruegel was in Rome during his Italian sojourn from 1552 to around 1554, he worked closely with Giulio Clovio (1498–1578), a manuscript illuminator skilled in grisaille.[20] Stained glass was another medium in which northern artists worked in partial or full grisaille. Bruegel may have retooled earlier drawn studies for that art form that feature a drummer and fifer in mercenary garb. References to stained glass—a medium where light transforms into an artistic material—add further meaning to the luminosity Bruegel achieved in *The Three Soldiers*.[21] Furthermore, as treated in detail below, with its pairing of muted palette and soldier subject, the Frick Bruegel responded to printmaking and other works on paper, due to the popularity of prints (and drawings) of mercenary soldiers.

Netherlandish painters from the first half of the sixteenth century took up divergent strategies when working in monochrome. One of these artists was the great inventor of hellscapes and demons, Hieronymus Bosch (ca. 1450–1516). Bosch worked in grisaille for the outer wings of enigmatic triptychs. His grisaille panels, such as those for the exterior of the *Temptation of St. Anthony* triptych (fig. 11) from the turn of the century, are painted narrative scenes devoid of color. The brushstrokes remain visible; Bosch did not blend them to imitate polished stone.[22] In contrast, the court artist Jan Gossart (ca. 1478–1532) sought new ways for his paintings to be in dialogue with sculptural models encountered locally and in Italy.[23] Only a year after Gossart's trip to Italy in 1508–9, he completed grisaille outer wings depicting the Penitent St. Jerome in the wilderness (fig. 12). The saint's drapery and the rocky outcroppings look carved. This visual effect, combined with Gossart's careful modulation of depth

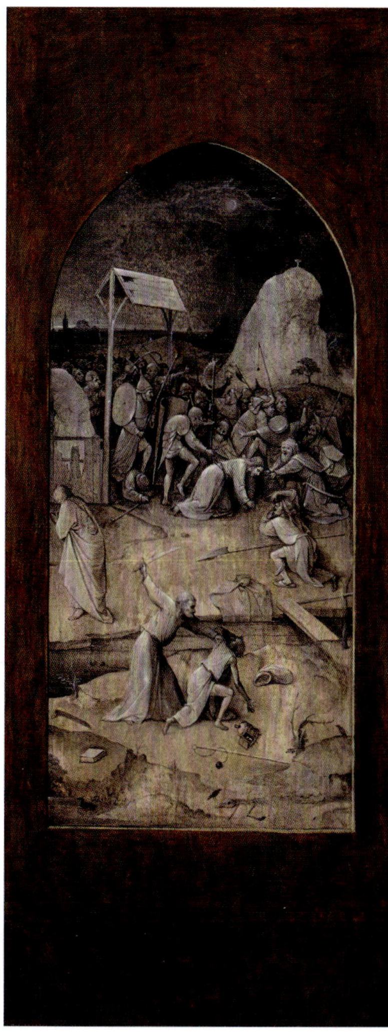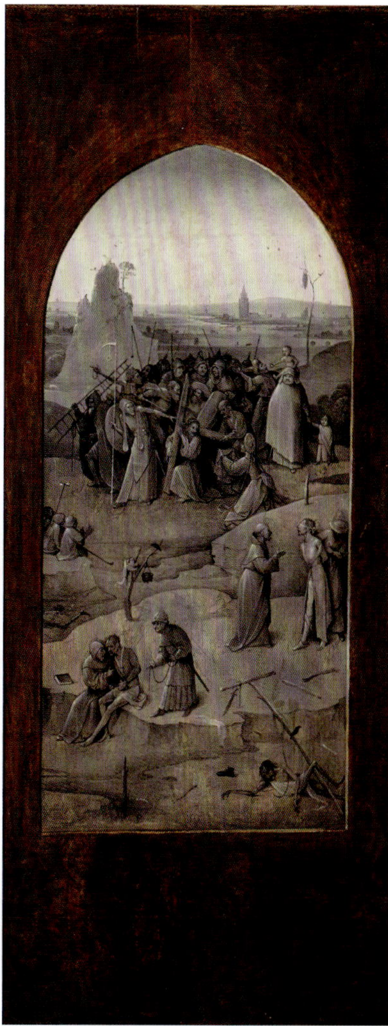

recession, succeeds in imitating the shallow relief sculpture (*rilievo schiacciato*) he would have encountered when he passed through Florence.[24]

A prime example of the synthesis of various Netherlandish approaches to grisaille painting is found on the outer wings of a monumental triptych painted by Pieter Coecke van Aelst (1502–1550) (fig. 13), Bruegel's father-in-law and likely teacher.[25] The outer wings of Coecke's triptych fit somewhere between Gossart and Bosch. Its details fall between trompe l'oeil imitation of low-relief sculpture and a tour-de-force demonstration of painterly qualities, as in the liquid flow of the drapery and clouds.

Fig. 11
Hieronymus Bosch
Temptation of St. Anthony
Triptych (closed view), ca. 1500
Oil on panel
51¾ × 20⅞ in. (131.5 × 53 cm) (each wing)
Museu Nacional de Arte Antiga, Lisbon

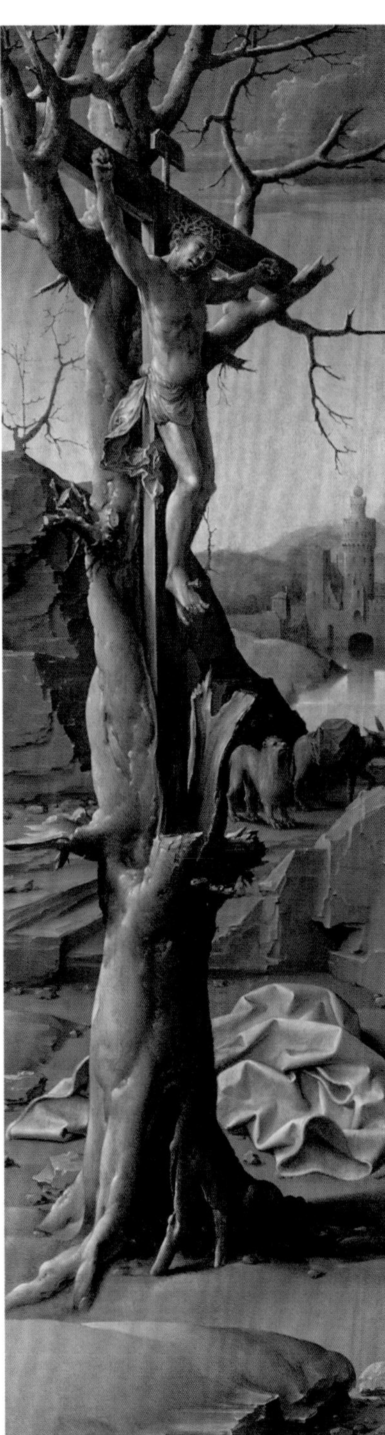

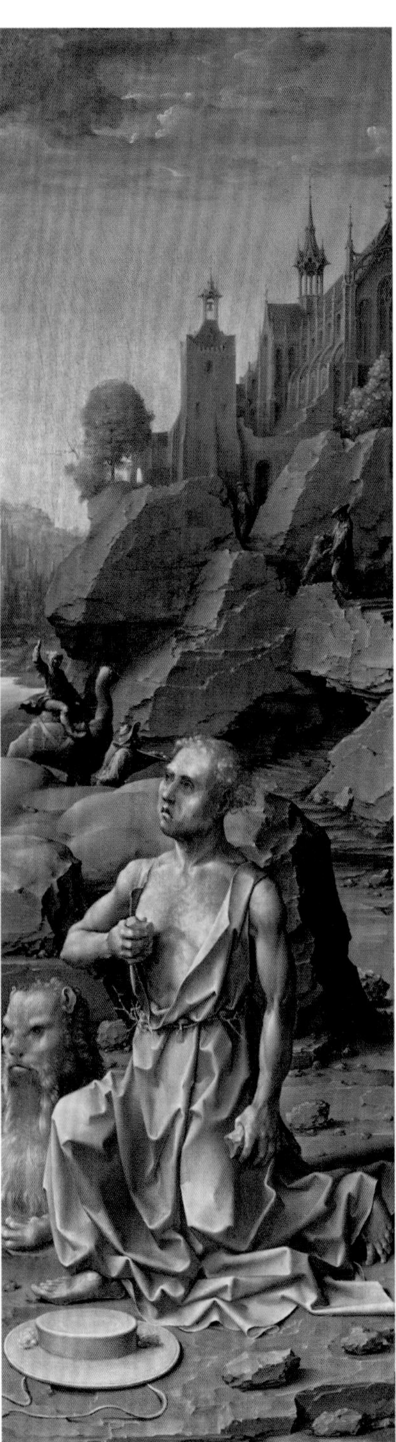

Fig. 12
Jan Gossart
Penitent St. Jerome, ca. 1510
Oil on panel
34⅛ × 9¹⁵⁄₁₆ in. (86.7 × 25.3 cm)
(each wing)
National Gallery of Art,
Washington; Samuel H. Kress
Collection

Fig. 13
Pieter Coecke van Aelst
Descent from the Cross Triptych
(closed view), ca. 1540–45
Oil on panel, 107⅞ × 33¹⁄₁₆ in.
(274 × 84 cm) (each wing)
Museu Nacional de Arte Antiga,
Lisbon

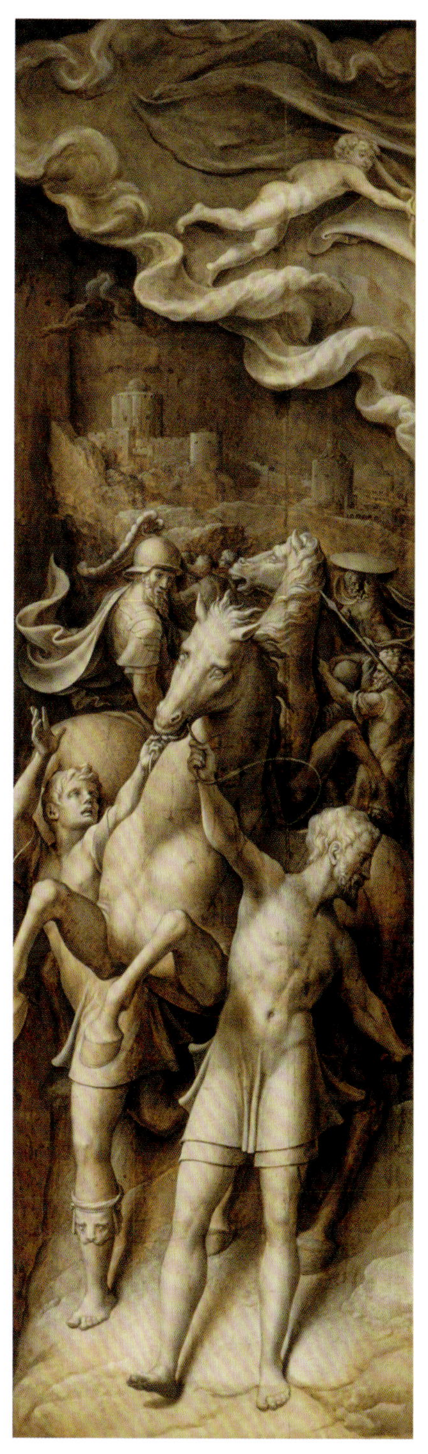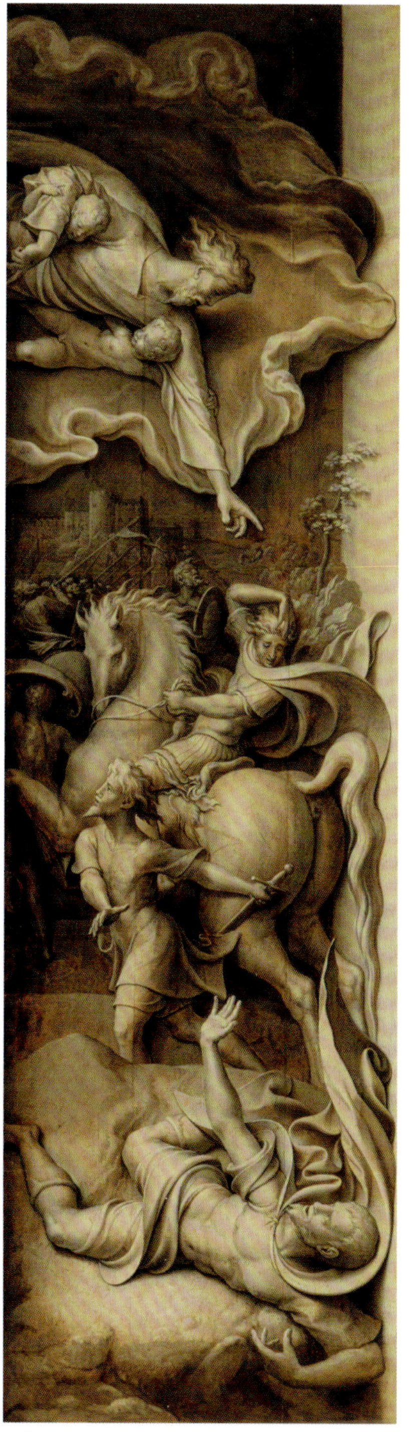

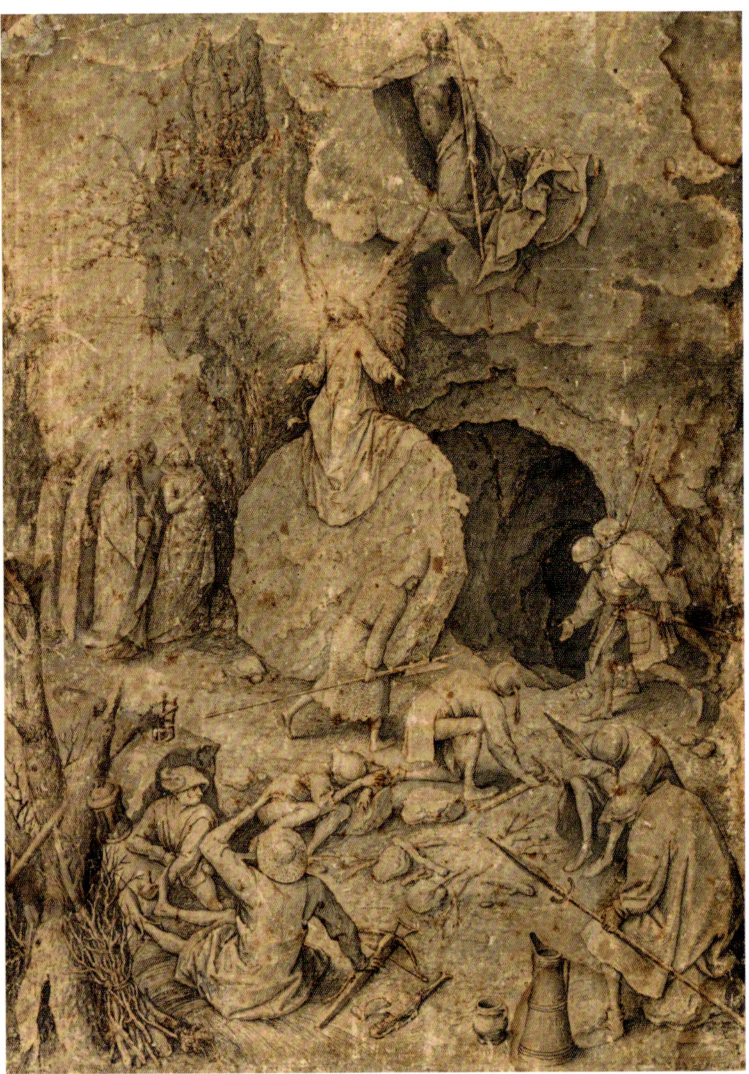

Fig. 14
Pieter Bruegel the Elder
Resurrection of Christ, ca. 1562
Pen and brown ink, brush and
gray ink, gray-blue wash, and
green bodycolor (traces)
17 × 12¹⁄₁₆ in. (43.1 × 30.6 cm)
Museum Boijmans Van
Beuningen, Rotterdam

One of Bruegel's competitors, the Antwerp painter Frans Floris (ca. 1519–1570), decorated his house with a facade (destroyed) that included painted imitations of bronze sculptures in niches. The facade also featured an allegorical scene that elevated painting, sculpture, and architecture to the status of the liberal arts. Informed by Italian theory, Floris's house decorations weighed in on local debates concerning the social status of practitioners. Placing painting in a *paragone* with sculpture through the inclusion of fictive bronzes stressed the intellectual dimensions of both art forms. It sought to elevate painters and sculptors above the house painters, furniture makers, and other craftsmen with whom they were traditionally grouped.[26]

Keeping close to Bosch's model, Bruegel specialized in painterly narrative scenes in black and white where the flourishes of his brush are evident.[27] Nevertheless, Bruegel would have appreciated the fuller Netherlandish tradition of grisaille and of the *paragone* between painting and sculpture in its manifold iterations. In his use of grisaille, Bruegel was an ingenious inheritor of multiple artistic traditions, both local and from Italy, and of a robust exchange with other media, reaching back to the artists and writers of antiquity as recorded by Pliny.[28]

Were the three paintings from the 1560s Bruegel's only grisailles? Of his extant works, there is debate about the *Resurrection of Christ* (fig. 14). Like the three grisaille paintings, this drawing is an autonomous work rather than a preparatory study. Contrasts between shadow and daylight play a large role in the scene, which takes place outside a cave at sunrise. Yet the blue-gray

Fig. 15
Jan Brueghel the Elder
Visit to the Farm, ca. 1600
Oil on panel
11¼ × 16¹³⁄₁₆ in.
(28.5 × 42.7 cm)
Fondation Custodia, Collection
Frits Lugt, Paris

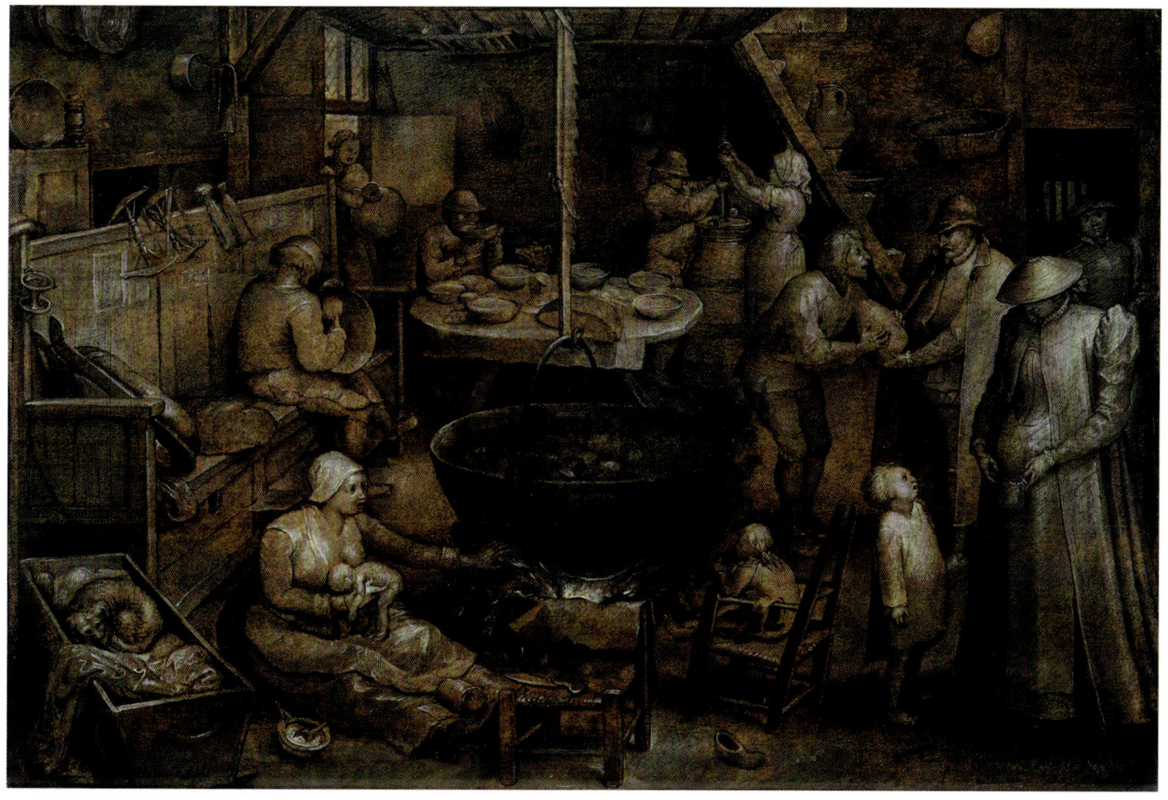

washes that lend the drawing its grisaille appearance may not be original.[29] Documentation points to other grisaille paintings by Bruegel, now lost. In 1550, Bruegel was commissioned to paint in black and white the outer wings of an altarpiece for St. Rumbold's Cathedral in Mechelen. Pieter Balten (ca. 1526–1584) was commissioned to paint the interior in color. A seventeenth-century Leiden inventory mentions a 1559 *Crucifixion* by Bruegel with exterior wings painted in oil in black and white.[30]

Two grisaille paintings titled *Visit to the Farm* are attributed to one of Bruegel's sons, Jan Brueghel the Elder (1568–1625) (fig. 15), and they may record a lost original by his father. At the very least, they represent a pastiche.[31] The paintings depict wealthy landowners visiting the full household of peasants who work their land. If a lost original by Pieter Bruegel the Elder of *Visit to the Farm* did exist, it would have been in good company with *The Three Soldiers*. Both are examples of genre subjects devoid of explicit religious, mythological, or historical content. Sixteenth-century Netherlandish genre painting—then an emerging and mutable category—catered to the urban elite yet focused on depictions of marginalized members of society, from rural peasants to mercenary soldiers from foreign lands.[32]

Bruegel's Audience

Nothing certain is known of the first owner of *The Three Soldiers*. The best insight into who the painting was intended for comes from the early ownership of Bruegel's other two extant grisaille paintings. The strong correspondences in dating, scale, technique, and quality point to all three works being created for similar viewers. Bruegel retained *Christ and the Woman Taken in Adultery* at the time of his death in 1569, almost five years after it was painted. It remained in the possession of Bruegel's family for decades thereafter. His painter sons Jan Brueghel the Elder and Pieter Brueghel the Younger (1564–1638), who were children when he died, went on to make numerous painted copies after it. Carried out in grisaille and translated into color, these copies attest to how greatly the original was valued.[33] The first recorded owner of the *Death of the Virgin* was Abraham Ortelius (1527–1598), an Antwerp cartographer, humanist, and avid collector of art whose friendship with Bruegel is well documented. The *Death of the Virgin* was in Ortelius's collection by 1574, the year he had a print made after it, engraved by Philips Galle (1537–1612) (fig. 16). These early reception histories of the *Death of the Virgin* and *Christ*

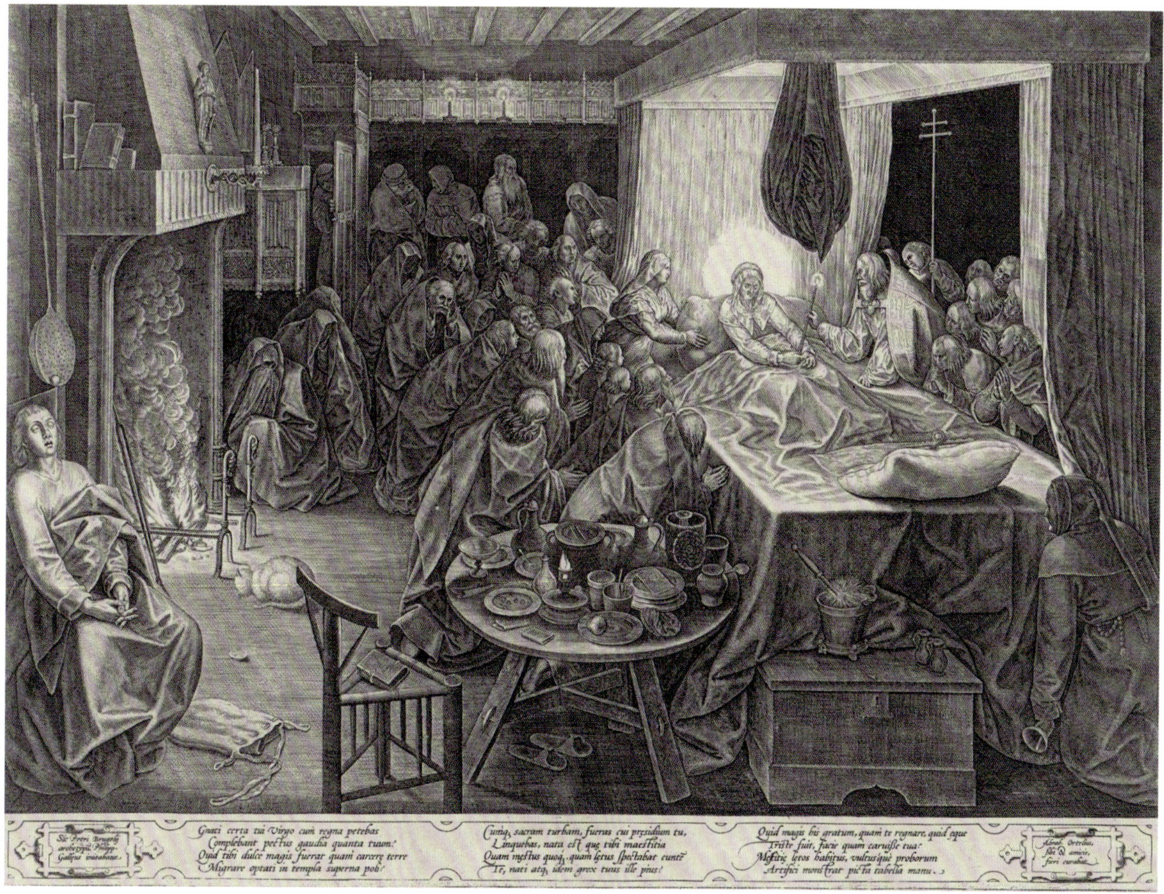

Fig. 16
Philips Galle after Pieter Bruegel
the Elder
Death of the Virgin, 1574
Engraving
12 3/16 × 16 7/16 in. (31 × 41.8 cm)
Rijksmuseum, Amsterdam

and the Woman Taken in Adultery indicate that all three intimately scaled and visually complex grisailles were made for the enjoyment of the artist himself and for a circle of well-educated individuals close to him.[34]

Along the bottom of the Galle print after the *Death of the Virgin* is an inscription detailing the circumstances of the print's commission. At left, the inscription attributes the design to Bruegel and names Galle as the printmaker. At right it reads, "On behalf of himself and his friends Abraham Ortelius took care of the production."[35] Ortelius commissioned the print to share it with a far-flung network. In 1578, Haarlem-based Dirck Volckertsz. Coornhert (1522–1590), who, among other things, was a playwright and printmaker, wrote to Ortelius thanking him for the gift. His phrasing supports the theory that Ortelius may have had a role in determining elements of the original

Fig. 17
Albrecht Dürer
Standard-Bearer, ca. 1499–1503
Engraving
4 9/16 × 2 13/16 in. (11.6 × 7.2 cm)
Rijksmuseum, Amsterdam

composition: "I do not think either [Bruegel or Galle] has ever done better. Thus their friend Abraham [Ortelius] with his favors encouraged both their arts."[36] As late as 1590, another member of the same circle, the Spanish theologian and humanist Benito Arias Montano (ca. 1527–1598), wrote to Ortelius asking for an impression of the print, which he received the following year.[37] What emerges from these letters is an image of the *Death of the Virgin* as a valued conversation piece among friends, one sustained over considerable time and geographic distance.[38]

When it comes to *The Three Soldiers*, a sophisticated original audience would likely have picked up on the elegance of the figures. The fifer's right hip juts out, his weight shifted to his right leg and his left foot lifting as he leans into a contrapposto pose, with a subtle *S*-curve to the dynamic stance. Twisting figures—and figures shown from different perspectives placed alongside one another (front and backside views)—competed with sculpture by demonstrating painting's ability to show figures in the round. Along with strong contrasts of light and dark (also found in *The Three Soldiers*), such figures were furthermore sought-after examples of contrasting formal elements, or *contrapposti* (antitheses), in Renaissance painting, identifiable to knowledgeable viewers.[39] Significantly, the drummer and fifer diverge from the stockier figure types with shorter limbs that audiences would expect from Bruegel (see, for example, fig. 26). In fact, in a 1565 "Invective," Lucas de Heere (ca. 1534–ca. 1584), who trained under Frans Floris, attacked Bruegel by characterizing the painter's figures as crude "carnival dolls" (*kaeremes poppen*) devoid of Italian or classical influences, Bruegel's time in Italy notwithstanding.[40] In this context, *The Three Soldiers* could be read in part as a rejoinder to contemporary critics who were skeptical of Bruegel's stylistic versatility and who missed the nuance of his selective assimilation of classicizing models.

Above all, the original audience of connoisseurs would have appreciated how *The Three Soldiers* responded to the well-established subject matter of *Landsknechte* or German mercenary soldiers. The German artist Albrecht Dürer (1471–1528) engraved his *Standard-Bearer* at the turn of the sixteenth century (fig. 17). Ortelius's collection contained impressions of almost all Dürer's prints. While not all of the prints owned by Ortelius were documented, the collection could very well have included the *Standard-Bearer*, which Bruegel then could have admired.[41] (Bruegel borrowed from Dürer's 1510 woodcut of the *Death of the Virgin* for his own version of the subject, perhaps

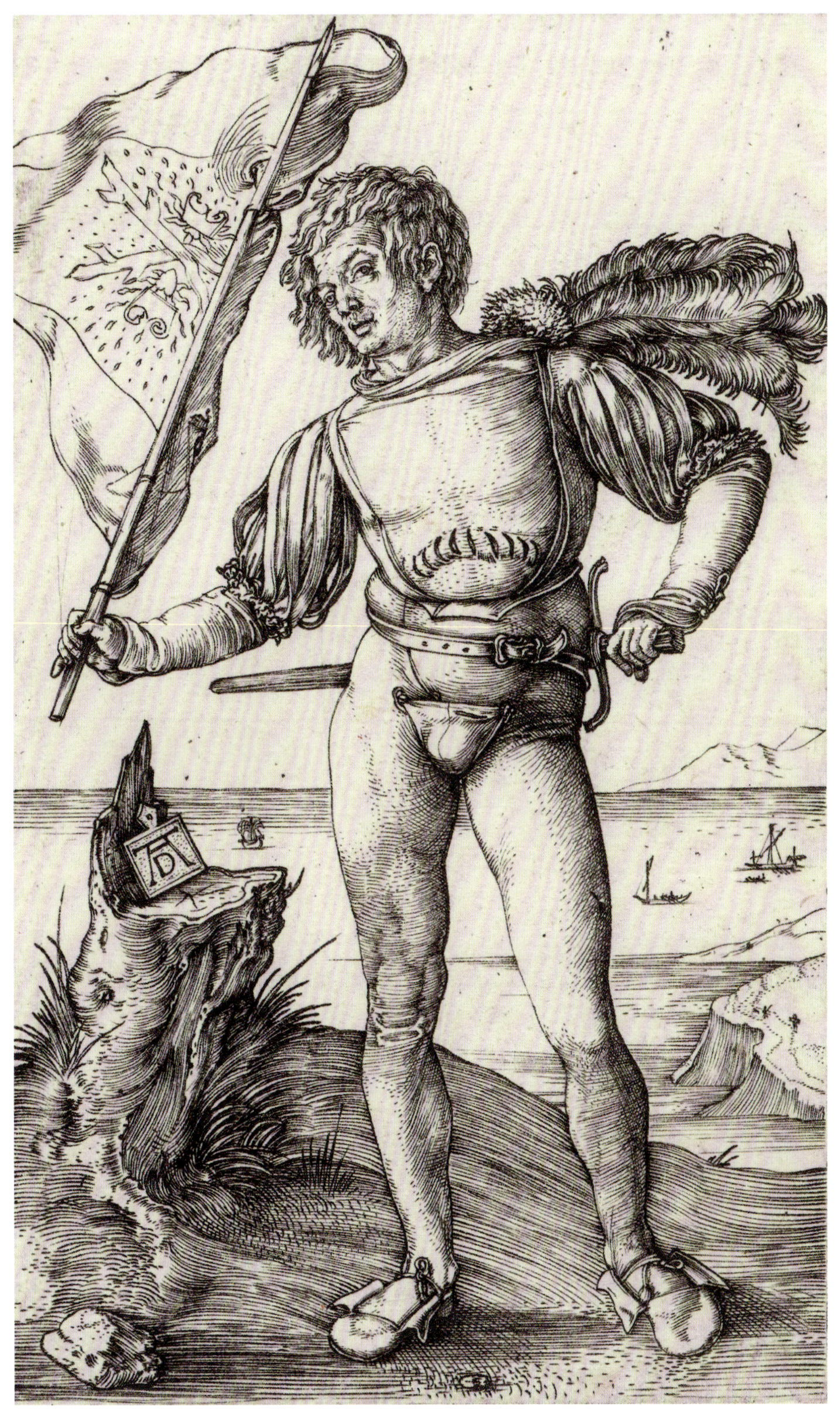

Fig. 18
Albrecht Altdorfer
Mercenary Foot Soldier, 1512
Pen and black ink heightened
with white gouache on paper
prepared with brown wash
5¹³⁄₁₆ × 4¹⁄₁₆ in. (14.8 × 10.3 cm)
The Frick Collection, New York;
Purchased by The Frick
Collection, 1936

studying an impression owned by Ortelius.) The significance of the mercenary subject for the first owner of Bruegel's painting deserves further exploration, first in its original artistic context—alongside Dürer's print and more local iterations of *Landsknechte*—and then in the political context of the year in which it was made.

Mercenaries in Art: Between Leisure and Risk

With head cocked and eyebrow raised, the soldier in Dürer's *Standard-Bearer* strikes a confident contrapposto pose that showcases his flexed leg muscles. His appearance is more jaunty than it is threatening. His flag and the feathered headdress tied at his back flutter in the wind. The flag carries the insignia of the Habsburg Holy Roman Emperor, whose territories then included both Germany and the Low Countries.

German and Swiss mercenaries were a popular subject in sixteenth-century northern European art, especially in drawings and in prints, gaining momentum around the turn of the century with artists like Dürer. Dürer's standard-bearer influenced Netherlandish artists already in the first decades of the 1500s, as evidenced by Lucas van Leyden's engraving (see fig. 5). Here the standard-bearer is just as energetic yet unhurried as the soldier in Dürer's prototype. Examples range from large-scale, multi-artist works that served as propaganda for the Habsburg Holy Roman Emperor to satirical depictions to more intimate artistic expressions. The Frick owns a sensitive drawing by Albrecht Altdorfer (ca. 1480–1538)—*Mercenary Foot Soldier* (fig. 18)—that is on colored prepared paper of about 6 by 4 inches. Along with Dürer, Altdorfer, and other German artists, the Swiss artists Niklaus Manuel Deutsch (1484–1530) and Urs Graf (ca. 1485–ca. 1529) are two prolific early contributors to the genre, specializing in drawings of military life. Both served as mercenaries themselves.[42]

When it comes to the propagandistic vein in German art, brave mercenaries bolstered the Holy Roman Emperor's military might. For example, in the Nuremberg woodcut series introduced above, a print by Erhard Schön (1491–1542) features a Swiss mercenary named Gall von Unterwalden (see fig. 3). In the accompanying poem by Hans Sachs (1494–1576), the depicted soldier proclaims his loyalty, which is to his homeland unless there is a righteous cause to fight abroad.[43] The admiring German visual culture around mercenary soldiers focused on infantry leaders, reflecting class hierarchies. Notably, this

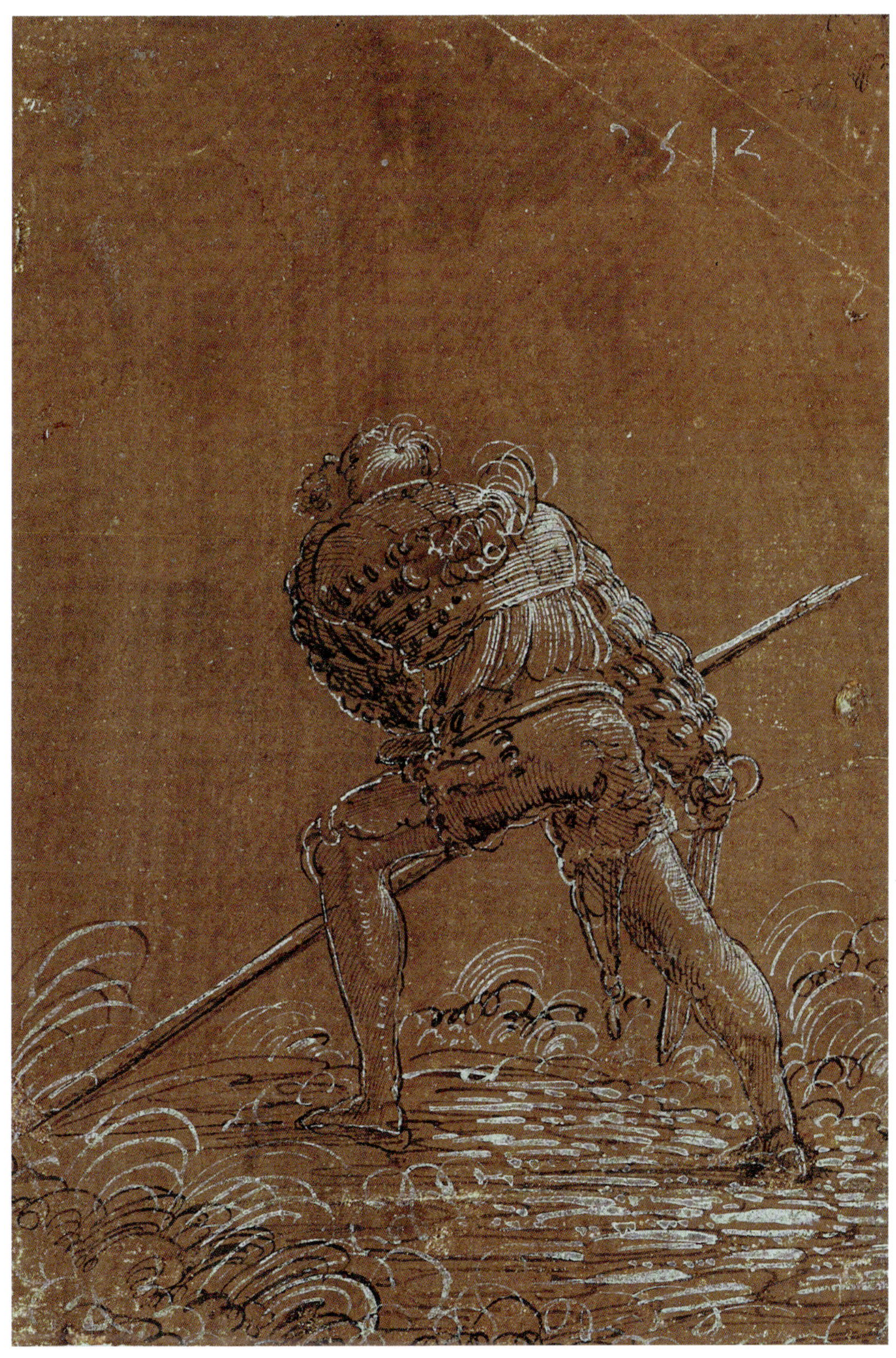

includes the familiar grouping of standard-bearer, fifer, and drummer, who led troops in combat. Due to their prominent and thus vulnerable place at the front of armies, those in these elite roles had a reputation for bravery.[44]

Not all German depictions were so adulatory. Even within the same Nuremberg woodcut series, viewers also encounter moralizing critiques of soldiers' behavior. More negative portrayals satirized mercenaries who were motivated by material gain. These representations take aim at artisans and urban laborers going to war. The biting tone caters to an upper-middle-class audience (such as merchants) who did not face the same difficult economic trade-offs. Another woodcut by Schön, again accompanied by a Sachs poem, depicts a shoemaker who, already having been to war, boasts to his sweetheart of the enrichment offered by reenlisting. Imagery of destitute mercenaries—with ironic titles like *Hanns Unverdorben* (John Unspoiled)—and their female companions returning home from war made clear that viewers should not take this promise of financial gain at face value. These returning soldiers have nothing to show for their service but wounds, disease, and torn uniforms.[45]

The foolish mercenary brought low is commonplace in the writings of the Dutch humanist Desiderius Erasmus (ca. 1469–1536). He decried mercenaries and their extravagant dress in terms similar to those of German moralists. In "The Soldier and the Carthusian," a dialogue in the *Colloquies* first published in 1523, Erasmus has an austere Carthusian monk interrogate a mercenary about his flashy appearance:

> How many colours are you painted with? No bird has such varied plumage. And then how slashed everything is, how unusual or outlandish! Add to that your haircut, half-shaven beard, and the tangled bush on your upper lip, sticking out on each side like a cat's whiskers.[46]

The comparison of the flamboyance of the mercenary's attire to feathers serves as another reminder of the colorfulness of the costuming that Bruegel chose to suppress in *The Three Soldiers*—not to mention the real ostrich and peacock feathers that adorned soldiers' headgear, including the drummer's hat in the Frick painting. The mustache that is "like cat's whiskers" parallels the draping mustache of the fifer in *The Three Soldiers*. Despite this memorable conjuring of an intricate costume and facial hair, in "The Soldier and the

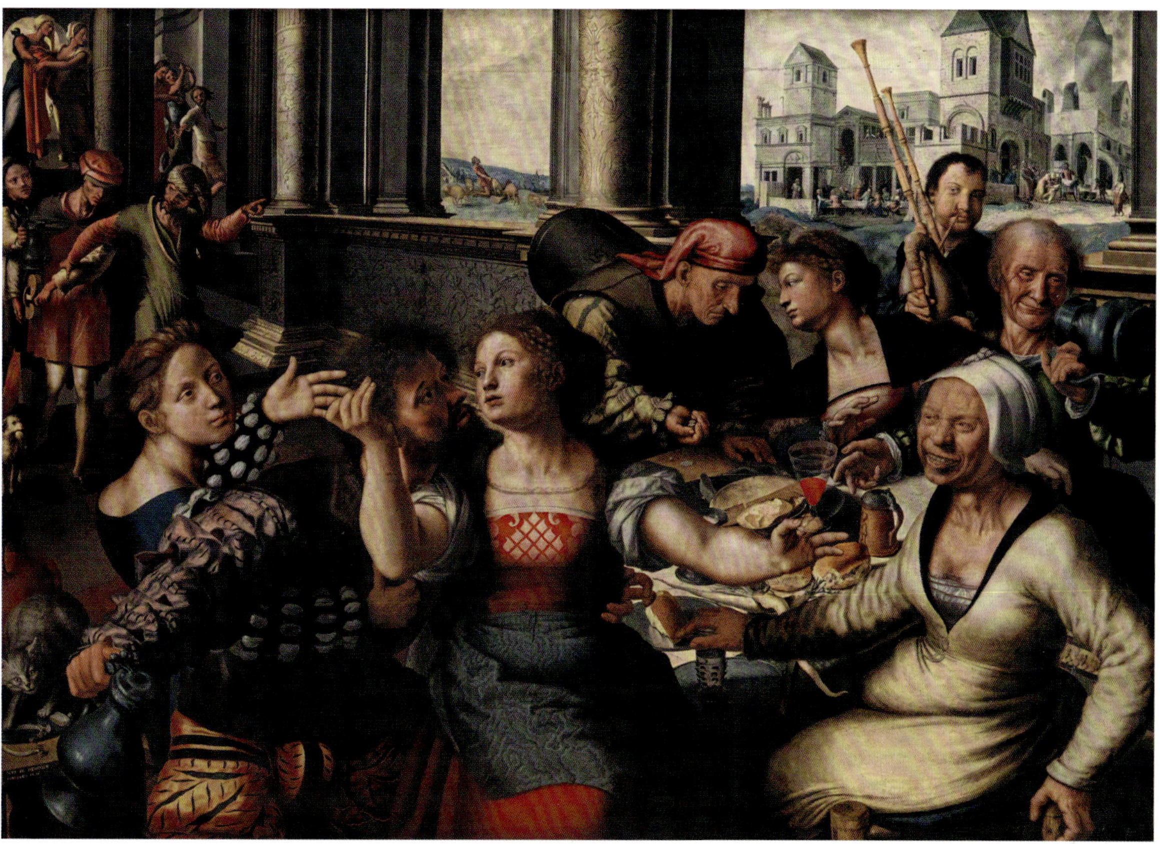

Fig. 19
Jan Sanders van Hemessen and
the Master of Saints Paul and
Barnabas (background vignettes)
The Prodigal Son in a Brothel,
1536
Oil on panel
55⅛ × 77¹⁵⁄₁₆ in. (140 × 198 cm)
Musées Royaux des Beaux-Arts,
Brussels; Acquired from Count
Edgar de Nécanda, Paris, 1881

Carthusian" and elsewhere in the *Colloquies*, Erasmus has mercenary soldiers voice the same conclusion warned about in prints like *Hanns Unverdorben*. The mercenary may have gone to war with hopes of enrichment, but he lost any earned or plundered wealth on "wine, whoring, and dice."[47] Ridicule is likewise elicited by dramatic portrayals. A Dutch play from the 1590s featured, in the titular role, a ridiculous mercenary "who fought against his own shadow." Unexpectedly, he loses the fight and must beg the audience to help subdue his opponent.[48]

In the generation before Bruegel, Netherlandish artists particularly developed the humorous aspects of soldiers at leisure. Their focus was on depicting off-duty soldiers spending their time and money in brothels, gambling and drinking (see fig. 4). Significantly, mercenary costume itself came to have distinctly bawdy connotations, serving as an attribute of dissipation. Take, for example, *The Prodigal Son in a Brothel* (fig. 19), a monumental painting by Jan

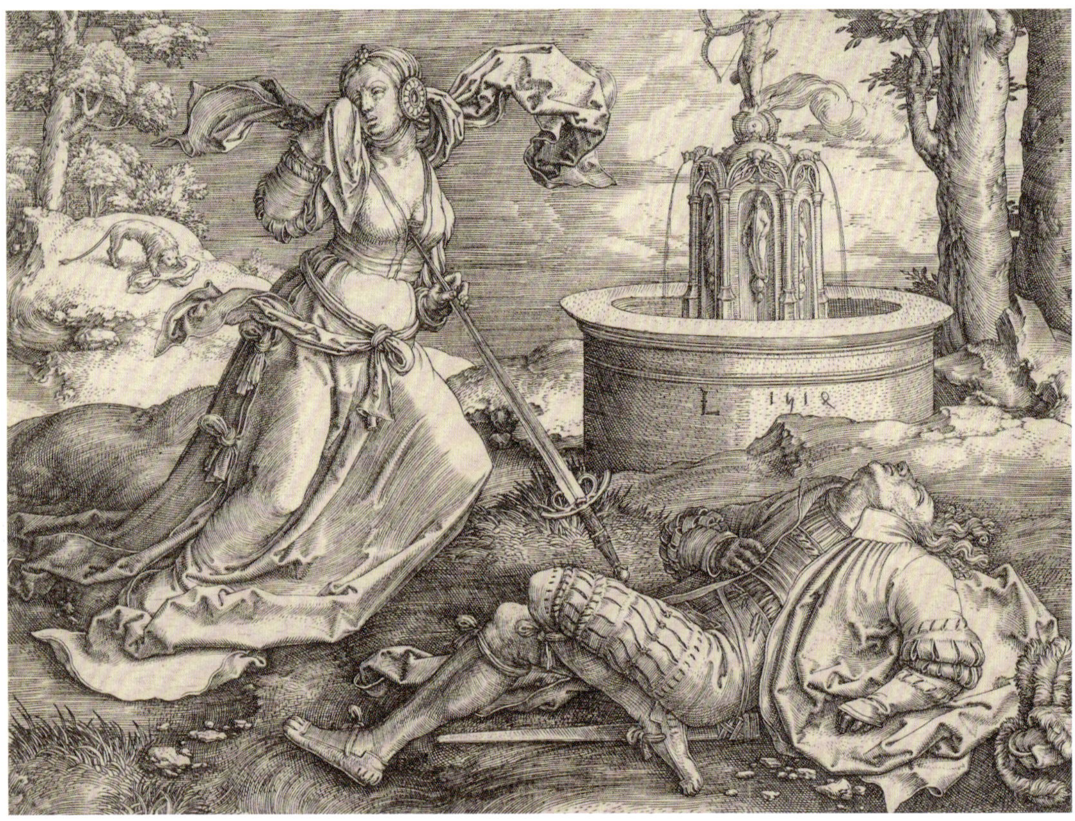

Fig. 20
Lucas van Leyden
Pyramus and Thisbe, 1514
Engraving
4 11/16 × 6 5/16 in. (11.9 × 16 cm)
The Metropolitan Museum of
Art, New York; Harris Brisbane
Dick Fund, 1934

Sanders van Hemessen (act. by 1524–d. after 1556), an Antwerp painter in the generation before Bruegel. (The background scenes were completed by a specialist known today as the Master of Saints Paul and Barnabas.) While it first appears to be a genre scene devoid of explicit religious content, it is a retelling of the Gospel parable (Luke 15:11–32) of the Prodigal Son's journey from sin to repentance and redemption. Van Hemessen focuses on the opening scenes of transgression. Dressed as a German mercenary, the Prodigal Son (at lower left) is imagined as wasting his father's fortune in a brothel. The costume's bright colors are boldly displayed. Thanks to the drunken Prodigal Son's splayed pose, so is his codpiece. References to classical narratives did not necessarily elevate the dress's connotations. In Lucas van Leyden's engraving of the Ovidian story of Pyramus and Thisbe (fig. 20), Thisbe kills herself with Pyramus's sword after she discovers her lover's dead body. The placement of the sword is no coincidence. Neither is the decision to dress Pyramus as a mercenary.[49]

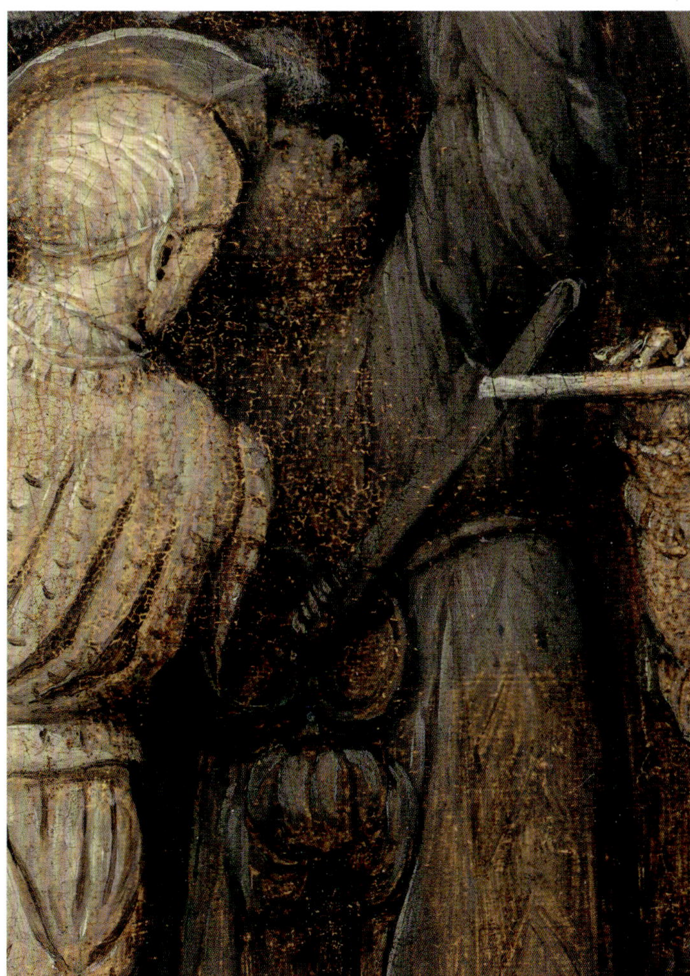

Fig. 21
Detail of Bruegel the Elder, *The Three Soldiers*, 1568 (frontispiece)

Fig. 22
Detail of Bruegel the Elder, *The Three Soldiers*, 1568 (frontispiece)

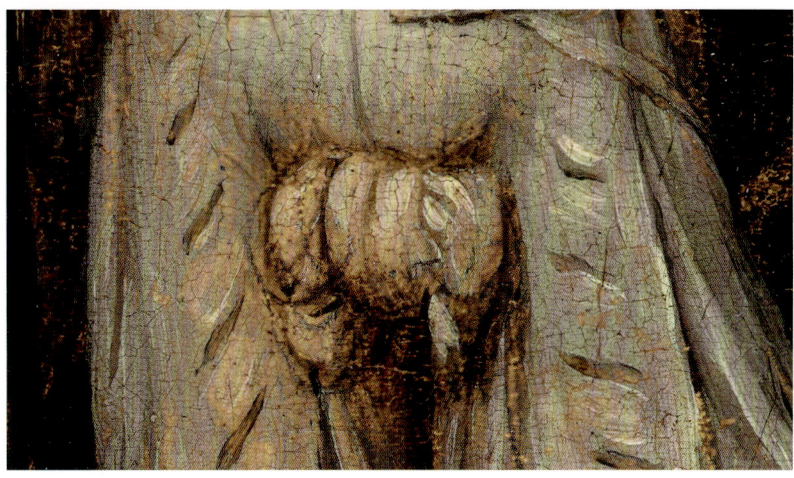

Fig. 23
Urs Graf
The Bearer of the Banner of the Canton Glarus, 1521
Pen and brown ink
11⁵⁄₁₆ × 7½ in. (28.8 × 19 cm)
The Metropolitan Museum of Art, New York; Promised Gift of Leon D. and Debra R. Black, and Purchase, Harris Brisbane Dick Fund, 2003

The standard-bearer in *The Three Soldiers* also has a sword that appears suggestively placed (fig. 21).[50] The standard-bearer and fifer wear *Pluderhosen*: long, baggy hose associated with German mercenaries. With *Pluderhosen*, the codpiece is bulked up by bow-like strips of lighter fabric sewn onto it, as Bruegel shows (fig. 22). German mercenaries' dress was exempt from sumptuary laws that curbed splendor and ornamentation in fashion based on social rank. Soldiers' dress therefore confounded class distinctions—one of the ways their attire was deemed risky. The looser fit of the hose may not look particularly provocative to us, but German moralists attacked *Pluderhosen* as a sign of the devil.[51]

Not just a cautionary figure, the type of the beautiful young soldier was something of a sixteenth-century sex symbol. The historian Ulinka Rublack describes "a slim, tall silhouette . . . idealized in the many presentations of hyper-fashionable and sexually attractive lansquenet soldiers."[52] When it comes to the representations considered above, this description refers more to Dürer's or Lucas van Leyden's prints of elite standard-bearers than to the satirical representations of the shoemaker or "Hanns Unverdorben." Therefore, indicators of class eluded by the mercenary dress are reinscribed based on the soldiers' rank and once again inflect the level of idealization or parody. The type described by Rublack is exemplified, furthermore, by a standard-bearer in tight hose and contrapposto stance shown from the back in a drawing by Urs Graf (fig. 23). It depicts a sporty, almost courtly masculinity embodied by a slender frame rather than a muscle-bound Hercules. As Rublack notes, this graceful type, whether celebrated or condemned, was understood as contrasting with another masculine physique—stockier, older—believed to typify upper-middle-class civic values of marriage and fatherhood. While the beauty of young soldiers with willowy, athletic builds and ornate fashions could be praised, as was their heroism in battle, they were also deemed transgressive for how—as itinerant, often unmarried men—they challenged traditional ideas of productive domesticity. Their rejection of a certain ideal of respectable, settled masculinity could be seen as alternately threatening or desirable.[53]

The drummer in Bruegel's painting likewise wears tight hose (albeit with slashes that obscure his buttocks and legs somewhat), and his turning body provides a backside view. Also taking into account the sinuous contours of the figures, the suggestive placement of the standard-bearer's sword, and the eye-catching codpiece of the fifer, Bruegel's homage to two distinct yet

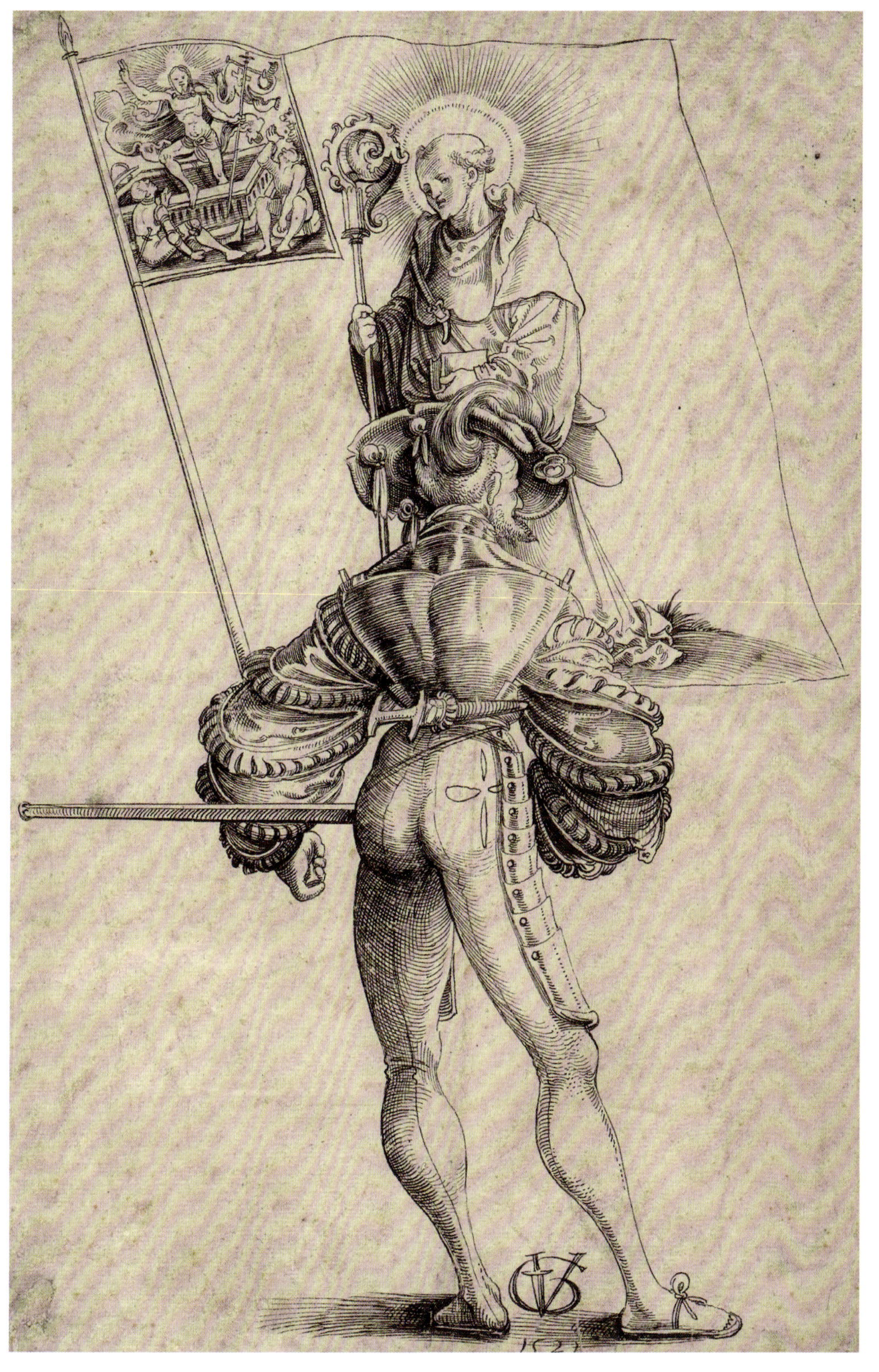

interconnected visual modes is discernible. The first is the tradition of bawdy Netherlandish depictions of mercenaries at leisure. The second is a more refined tradition that focuses admiringly on the bodies of elite soldiers as accentuated by their attire. Soldiers in tight hose, as in the Graf drawing, provided sixteenth-century artists with ample opportunities to study muscular male bodies in a range of poses, especially backside views.[54] Patricia Rubin writes, "In play here . . . is the allure of the male body as the subject and object of art. At stake is the way the admiring artist's skill at creating admirable masculinity can suggest the erotic."[55] At the very least, such depictions undeniably render the soldier's body with care, encouraging viewers to linger on the portrayal with appreciation of its beauty.

Textual documentation of same-sex desire in early modern Dutch (as well as German and Swiss) sources mostly centers around accusations and trials in a culture where sodomy was criminalized.[56] The rarer textual references outside of this repressive framework include a noteworthy instance connected to the *Landsknechte* visual tradition. In a letter of September 8, 1506, from Venice to his friend and patron Willibald Pirckheimer (1470–1530), Dürer exclaimed, "Oh, if only you were here! [H]ow you would like these fine Italian soldiers!" While the lines are ambiguous, the teasing intimacy recorded throughout the correspondence suggests sexual innuendo.[57] In the much more numerous court cases, public defamations, and political propaganda, mercenary soldiers were often accused of sodomy, as a specific iteration of their general reputation for promiscuity and as a political tactic against the foreign governments they served.[58] For example, a 1574 song in a Dutch songbook characterizes Habsburg armies, which included German mercenaries, as full of "whoremongers and sodomites."[59] The songbook is full of pro-Dutch songs created during the early years of the Dutch Revolt against the Habsburgs.

To sum up, in early modern northern Europe, soldiers—already framed as licentious—were at times negatively associated with sodomy in contemporaneous texts. As already suggested by the slur from the 1574 song, the ribald brothel scenes with soldiers (see figs. 4, 19) were not so far from these admonitory depictions of same-sex desire. Both fell under an umbrella of non-reproductive sex by period definitions of sex outside of traditional Christian structures of marriage and inheritance.[60] Yet, while the textual evidence from the period (be it criminal records or propaganda) primarily reflects a repressive cultural climate, the visual tradition of beautiful male soldiers in extravagant but revealing

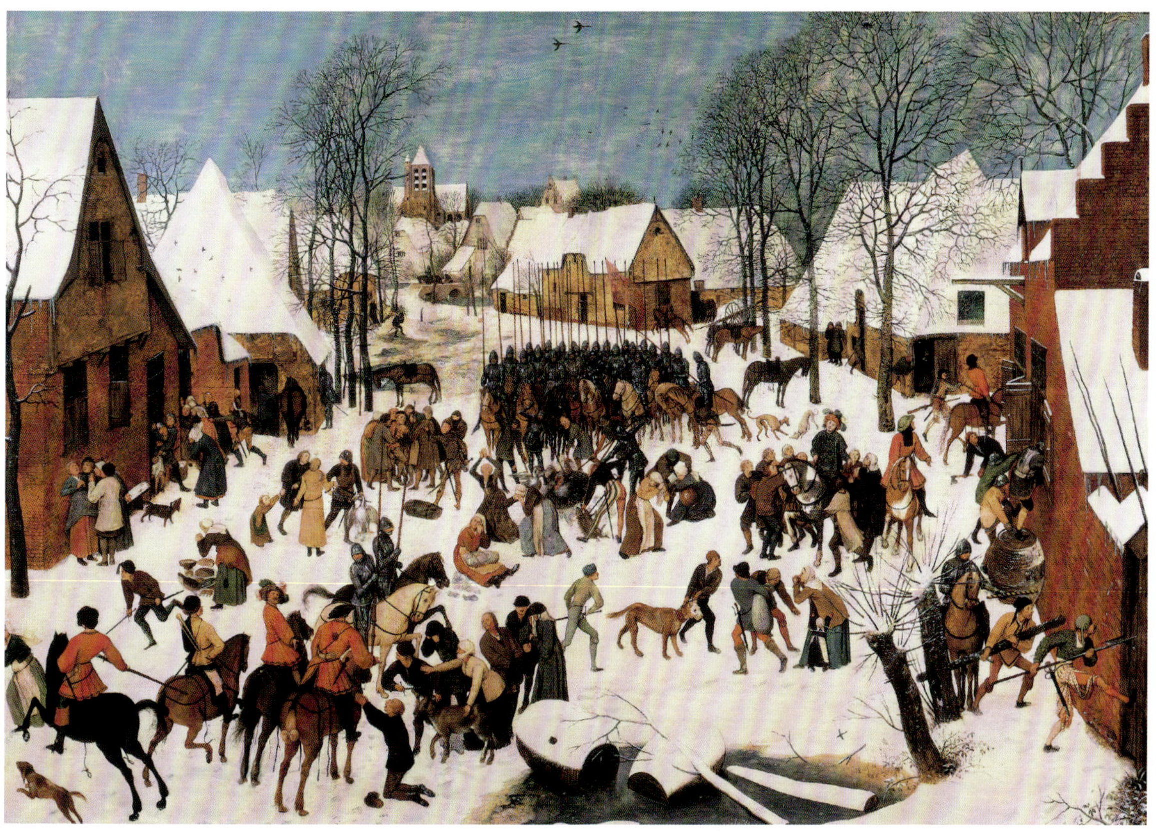

Fig. 24
Pieter Bruegel the Elder
Massacre of the Innocents,
ca. 1565–67
Oil on panel
43 × 62¼ in. (109.2 × 158.1 cm)
Royal Collection Trust, Windsor
Castle, Windsor

dress can offer avenues for recuperating some sense of the homosocial or even homoerotic dimensions of representations of soldiers outside of the arenas of early modern law and politics. They invite an admiring, if not outright desiring, gaze from viewers—including, though not exclusively, men.[61]

In general, this type of representation focused on male beauty is most prevalent in art before 1550; Dürer's famous *Standard-Bearer* is from the turn of the century. The outfits, too, appear outdated in Bruegel's *Three Soldiers*. While German mercenary soldiers were still very active in 1568, at the outset of the Dutch Revolt—as discussed below—military attire had changed. The bright red coats of contemporary Habsburg soldiers appear in Bruegel's *Massacre of the Innocents* (fig. 24).[62] A closer look at the circumstances of the year Bruegel created *The Three Soldiers* sheds further light on his intriguing reworking of *Landsknechte* as personifications of a certain type of military masculinity, in outdated dress from the time of Dürer's print.

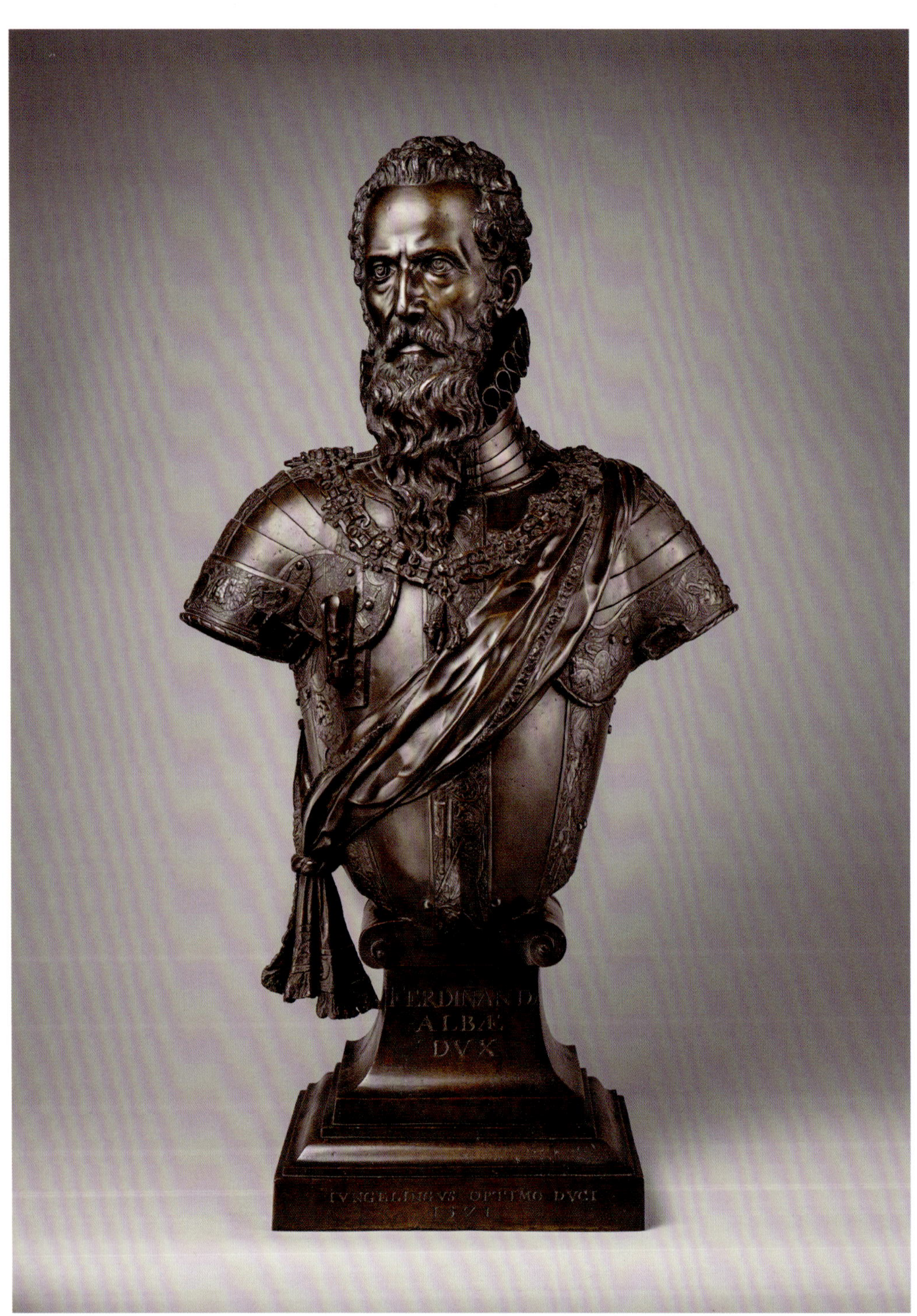

FERDINANDVS
ALBÆ
DVX
IVNGELINGVS OPTIMO DVCI
1571

The Year 1568

In 1568, war loomed. Therefore Bruegel's choice of military subject was not a theoretical one. It must be considered in the context of the Dutch Revolt against Habsburg rule, which began in that year.[63] Fernando Álvarez de Toledo (1507–1582), the Duke of Alba, arrived in Brussels in August 1567 in the capacity of governor-general of the Netherlands under the Habsburg ruler Philip II (1527–1598). A rare portrait bust by Jacques Jonghelinck (1530–1606) captures his severe visage (fig. 25). Dubbed the "Butcher of Flanders" by his enemies, the Duke of Alba led the brutal suppression of the revolt. His appointment in 1567 was in response to the events of 1566—the so-called "wonder year" (*wonderjaar* or *annus mirabilis*). It was, among other things, a year of iconoclasm, when anti-Catholic crowds destroyed public religious art, condemning it as idolatrous.[64]

The defining events leading to outright war in 1568 were shaped by Protestant beliefs—exemplified by the 1566 iconoclasm led by Calvinists—that had been simmering in Southern Netherlandish cities since at least the 1530s, despite suppression by the staunchly Catholic Habsburgs. Yet they were equally defined by the grievances of local aristocrats and civic leaders who felt their longstanding guarantees of partial self-governance had been impinged upon by Habsburg authorities.[65] Their resistance to carrying out Habsburg edicts against Protestant "heretics" did not necessarily reflect local authorities' own religious sympathies. Instead, their protection of rights of self-governance was paired with an acute awareness of how religious intolerance negatively impacted the international mercantile economy of a highly urbanized region.[66]

The Duke of Alba's response to the 1566 "wonder year" only intensified hostilities. His approach of spectacular punishment is best illustrated by a particular bloody event in 1568: the public execution in Brussels (where Bruegel was based at the time) of two members of the local nobility, the counts of Egmont and Horne, on July 5. Egmont and Horne had opposed the iconoclasm and considered themselves loyal to Philip II. It was a move that shocked contemporaries, and it was ultimately fatal to Alba's aims of bringing the Low Countries to heel. In the aftermath of these executions, the Dutch nobleman William of Orange (1533–1584) prepared to lead a military invasion of the duchy of Brabant in that year.[67]

Given the explosive political situation in the last years of Bruegel's life, scholars have interpreted enigmatic images created by the artist in the 1560s

Fig. 25
Jacques Jonghelinck
Don Fernando Álvarez de Toledo, Third Duke of Alba, 1571
Bronze
46 × 26¾ × 15 in.
(116.8 × 67.9 × 38.1 cm)
The Frick Collection, New York

in political terms.[68] These include several works also dating to 1568, such as the *Magpie at the Gallows* (fig. 26), a small-scale landscape painting, where peasants dance—and defecate—near the eponymous gallows, seeming to laugh in the face of death. The peasants have been interpreted alternately as figures of derision or as covert "avatars of Netherlandish identity" resisting Habsburg rule. In Joseph Koerner's words, they express "dangerously defiant recognition that law and authority," represented by the gallows, "being human forms, can legitimately be resisted."[69] One of Bruegel's versions of

Fig. 26
Pieter Bruegel the Elder
Magpie at the Gallows, 1568
Oil on panel
18¹⁄₁₆ × 20 in. (45.9 × 50.8 cm)
Hessisches Landesmuseum,
Darmstadt

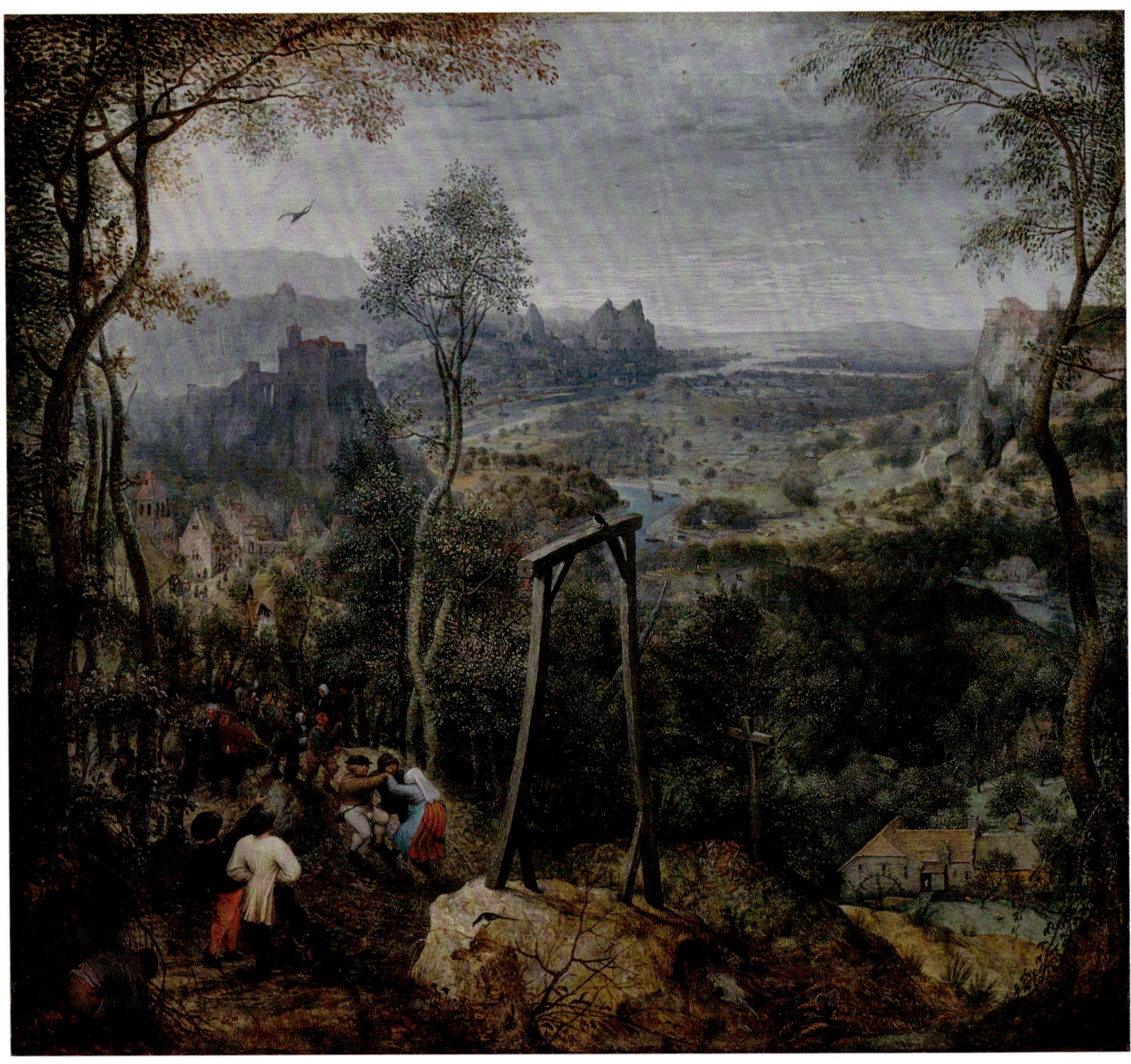

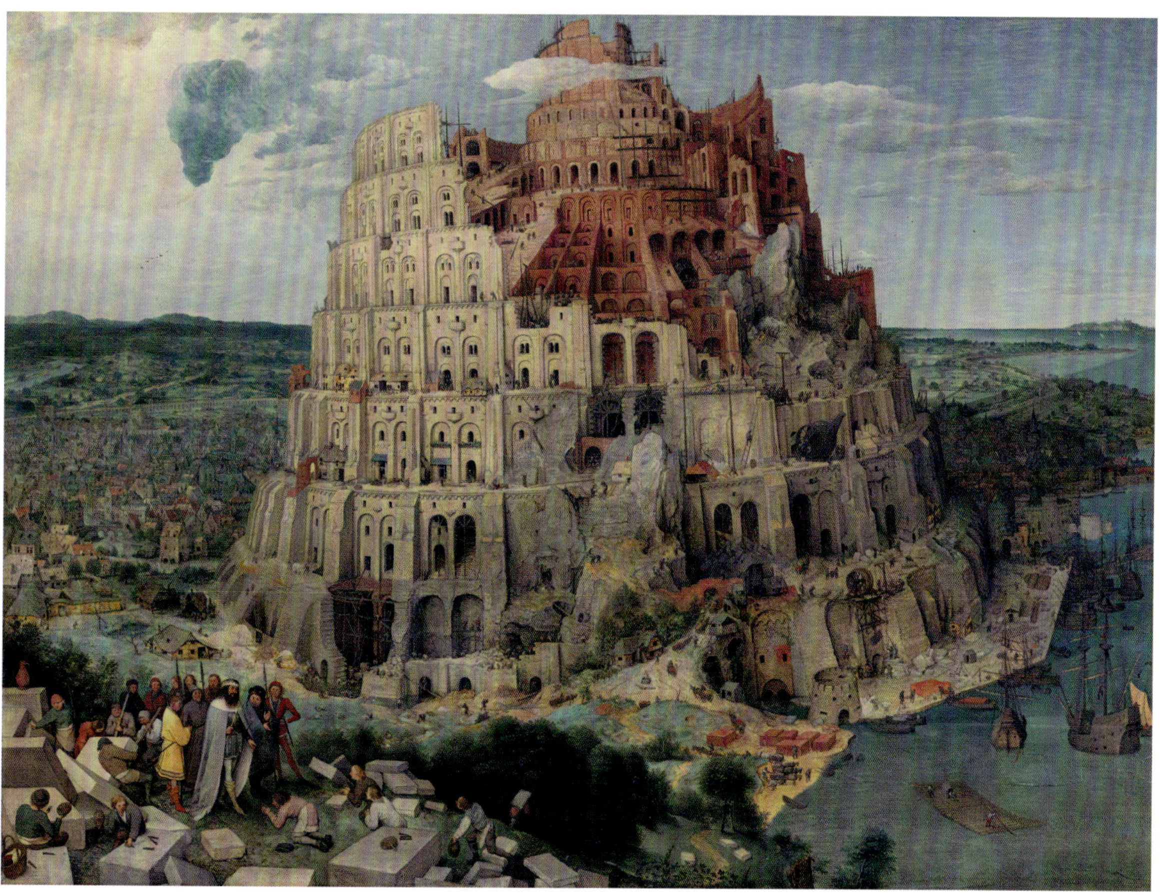

the *Tower of Babel* (fig. 27) has recently been analyzed as a warning against political hubris implicating Philip II or as an allegory of iconoclasm.[70] The art historian Koenraad Jonckheere contends that the choice of grisaille technique for the *Death of the Virgin* and *Christ and the Woman Taken in Adultery* may anticipate accusations of idolatry and the 1566 iconoclasm. Above all, through the suppression of one of painting's most alluring and life-like qualities—color—Bruegel's religious grisaille paintings actively resist any conflation by viewers of the depicted figures with the actual sacred personages they represent.[71]

Larry Silver argues that in contrast to Bruegel's customary depiction of soldiers as threatening (as in the *Massacre of the Innocents*, for example), *The Three Soldiers* represents an admission by the artist of the necessity of military force for resisting Alba's regime.[72] According to Silver, the outdated costuming

Fig. 27
Pieter Bruegel the Elder
Tower of Babel, 1563
Oil on panel
45 × 61¹⁄₁₆ in.
(114.3 × 155.1 cm)
Gemäldegalerie, Kunsthistorisches
Museum, Vienna

Fig. 28
Frans Floris
Awakening of the Arts, ca. 1559
Oil on canvas
63¾ × 94 in. (161.9 × 238.8 cm)
Museo de Arte, Ponce; The Luis
A. Ferré Foundation, Inc.

is Bruegel's attempt through historical distance "to claim deniability, personal detachment from the current controversies, if he were ever challenged."[73] Silver's reading rightly seeks a way to connect the soldier iconography to the start of the Dutch Revolt while offering an explanation for the fact that the soldiers lack menace.[74]

To further complicate matters, German mercenaries were hired to fight on both sides of the Dutch Revolt.[75] Moreover, in Bruegel's painting, the figures are isolated from the rest of their infantry unit, appearing in an undefined, shadowy space. They may be military leaders, but they seem poised to circle one another as figures of diversion rather than action. *The Three Soldiers*, then, presents a seeming paradox. On one hand, the closer one studies the delicate composition, the more it resists the notion that Bruegel might be weighing in on the developing conflict. On the other hand, it is difficult to imagine that Bruegel's choice of military subject had nothing to do with the destabilizing political events unfolding in 1568. Put another way, presenting the mercenary subject as *removed* from the arena of real conflict was itself a meaningful choice in 1568.

To better understand this celebration of refined painterly technique, sumptuous costuming, and graceful male bodies, with its martial pageantry yet conspicuous lack of references to the realities of a region on the eve of war, it is helpful to return to the question of the original audience for *The Three Soldiers*. In sixteenth-century Europe, learned humanist culture had a strong pacifist bent and an aversion to extremism on both ends of the religious and political spectrum. Writing in 1567, Ortelius lamented the "disordered time" in which he and his friends found themselves. He blamed the destructive forces of both Catholic dogmatism and Calvinist zealotry.[76] As we have seen, the likely intended audience for *The Three Soldiers* was a small group of learned viewers, not unlike Ortelius, with at least some humanist training—a community of which Bruegel himself was a part.

The *Awakening of the Arts* (fig. 28), a monumental oil-on-canvas painting by Bruegel's contemporary Frans Floris, speaks to humanist anti-war commitments. Created around 1559 to mark the conclusion of another conflict—the Treaty of Cateau-Cambrésis, ending hostilities between Philip II and the French king Henry II (1519–1559)—it is an allegory of peace. The slumbering nude women in the foreground are allegorical personifications of the liberal arts. At lower right, the legible music of an open songbook

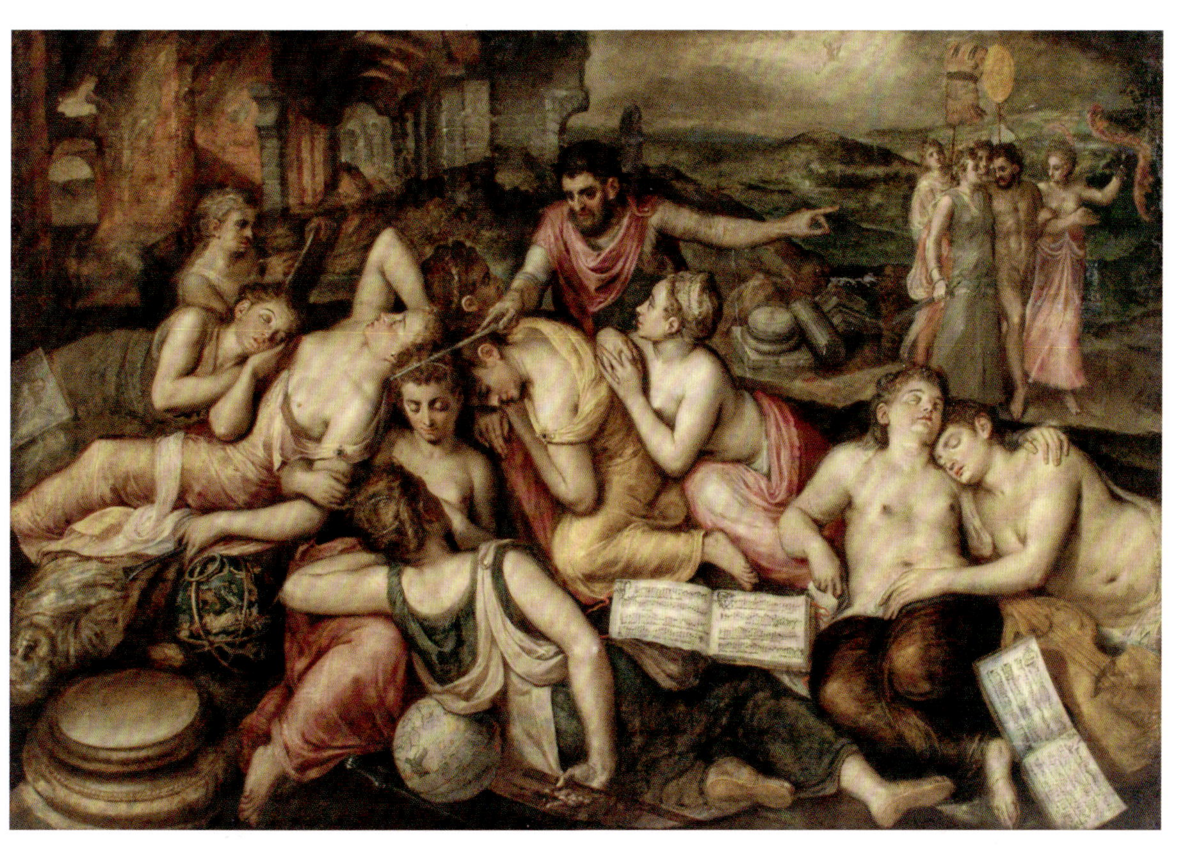

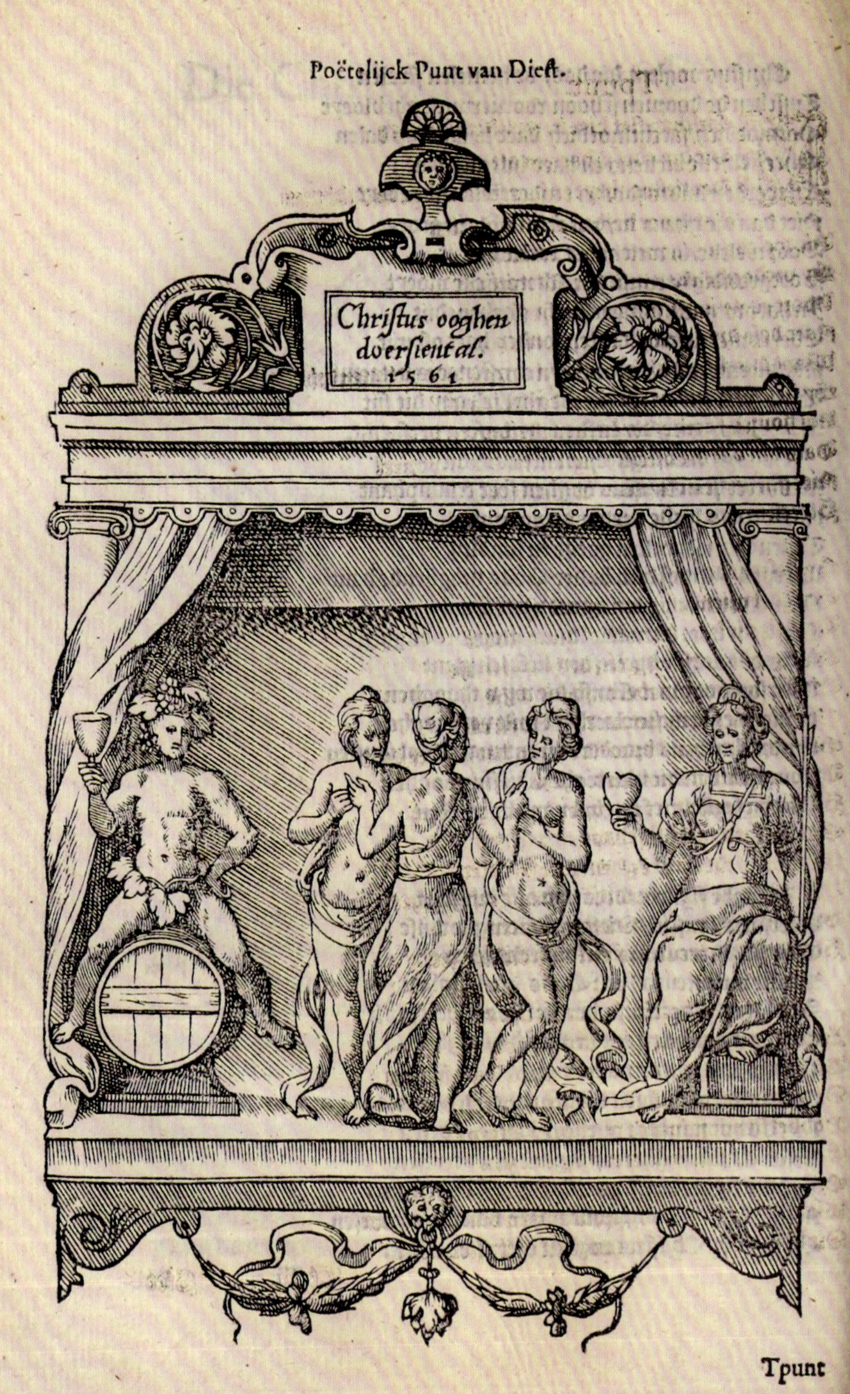
Chriſtus ooghen
doerſient al.
1561

reads: "The cruel Mars forces all sciences [all knowledge]/ To fall into a longer slumber/ But he has been defeated by prudence and by fortitude,/ And the True Friend will come to awaken us."[77] Mars, the god of war, is led away at upper right by female personifications of the Cardinal Virtues (including Prudence and Fortitude), stripped of his armor and weapons. The "True Friend" is Mercury, the god who oversees commerce and prosperity. Crowned by a laurel wreath, he bends down to awaken the sleeping women.

Floris's painting was commissioned by Niclaes Jonghelinck (1517–1570), a wealthy Antwerp merchant and banker who also owned the *Tower of Babel* (see fig. 27) and a number of other important paintings by Bruegel. (He was also the brother of Jacques Jonghelinck, who created the *Alba* bust [see fig. 25].) The *Awakening of the Arts* speaks to Jonghelinck's humanist aspirations. The message is that the liberal arts—including the visual arts in Floris's formulation (once again elevating painting, sculpture, and architecture according to period valuations)—depend on peace to flourish. Notably, Floris shows a moment of transition from war to peace, with classicizing ruins smoldering in the background of the stage-like space. Therefore, the *Awakening of the Arts* commemorates peace while warning of its precariousness. Peace must be vigilantly maintained.[78]

The necessity of peace for the pursuit of creative and intellectual endeavors was discussed at length in a series of performances held in 1561 by literary and dramatic societies known as chambers of rhetoric. The occasion was a *landjuweel* (literary competition) among chambers representing different cities in the duchy of Brabant. The competition took over the city of Antwerp for the month of August, drawing large crowds. It was hosted by an Antwerp chamber of rhetoric, De Violieren, which was housed in the painters' Guild of St. Luke, of which Bruegel was a member. The resulting productions had a strong visual component due to the ample use of tableaux vivants. Taking place in the wake of the Treaty of Cateau-Cambrésis, the performances spoke obliquely to contemporary political events, drawing heavily on mythological and biblical imagery.[79]

Classicizing poetic pageants performed as part of the competition examined the theme of "unyielding peace" (*Vrede onbeswijckelijck*) and the prosperity it brings.[80] A pageant by the chamber De Christusogen from the city of Diest took up the mythological subject of the Three Graces. In the woodcut illustration of the performance, the Graces encircle one another

Fig. 29
Woodcut of the Three Graces, illustrating the poetic pageant of De Christusogen (Diest). From the Silvius edition of *De Antwerpse spelen van 1561* (Antwerp, 1562). Getty Research Institute, Los Angeles

(fig. 29). Their braided limbs recall how peace is repeatedly described in the introductory poem in a refrain that concludes each stanza, as "strong . . . like a rope woven with three strands."[81] As this representation and the intertwined nude female personifications in Floris's painting suggest, central to both the *Awakening of the Arts* and to the public performances of the 1561 *landjuweel* were humanist themes of harmony, also underscored by the open book of music in Floris's painting.[82]

With the soldiers' dancer-like, circling poses and their music, harmony is also manifested by *The Three Soldiers*. Taking contemporaneous anti-war humanist discourse into account, what is ultimately most convincing, perhaps, is the idea that in *The Three Soldiers* Bruegel expresses both an admission of the necessity of military force to resist the Alba regime and, at the same time, a desire for the *Landsknechte* subject to remain an *artistic* one. The grisaille technique heightens this sense of the subject as emphatically artistic, given grisaille's long tradition of artistic competition and exchange across media. Furthermore, by drawing on both the bawdy and admiring approaches to the *Landsknechte* subject, Bruegel furthers the visual culture of mercenaries at leisure—even if standard-bearer, fifer, and drummer are indeed military leaders. He explores themes of masculinity, elegance, and playfulness with soldiers shown removed from imminent violence. Through its commitment to harmony and beauty in a discordant time, *The Three Soldiers* is saturated with a lyrical melancholy, as well as resistance to the damage war inflicts on creative and intellectual pursuits. It expresses a wish for art to be about artmaking in a time when painting, sculpture, and other liberal arts were destined not to awaken but to go into hibernation.

Afterlives

Nothing is known about the fortunes of *The Three Soldiers* for the rest of the sixteenth century. In the first half of the seventeenth century, the painting became part of the celebrated art collection of the English monarch Charles I (1600–1649). The mark *CP* topped by a crown branded on the reverse of the oak panel (fig. 30) stands for Carolus Princeps (Prince Charles), indicating that the painting came into Charles I's possession before his accession to the throne in 1625, when he was still Prince of Wales.[83]

The Three Soldiers is inventoried in Abraham van der Doort's (ca. 1575–1640) 1639 register of the king's collection as "Item painted in black

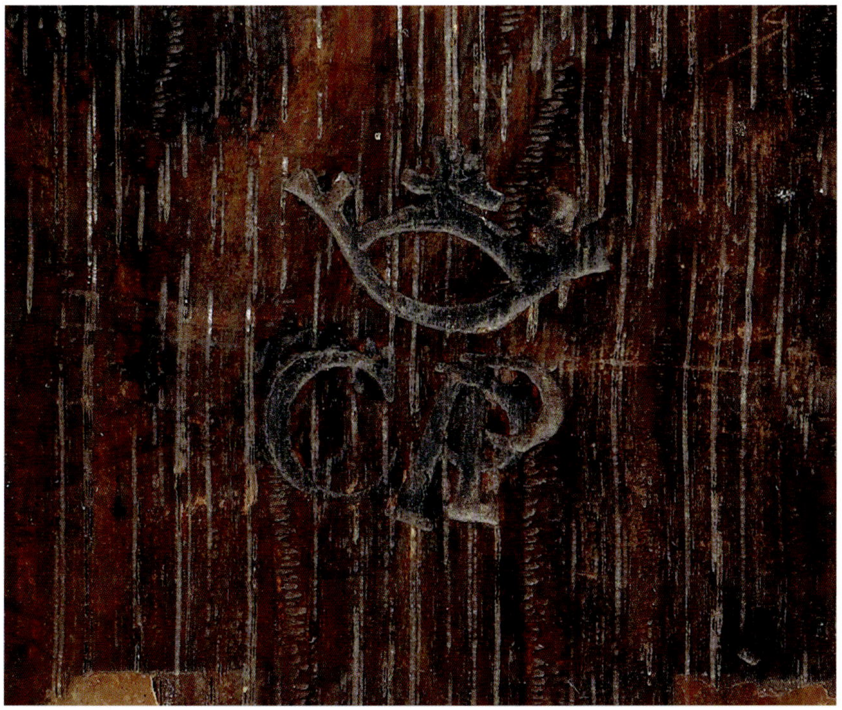

Fig. 30
Detail of the back of Bruegel the
Elder, *The Three Soldiers*, 1568
(frontispiece)

and white oyle Cullo[rs]/ upon a board" with a "gilded frame." Multiple
copies of the register survive. In the entry quoted above, the painting is
inaccurately ascribed to "y[e] young Brugill" and listed as a gift to the king.[84]
This erroneous attribution refers to Pieter Bruegel the Elder's son, Pieter
Brueghel the Younger, who devoted his career to copying his father's work.
Another copy of the register gives the correct attribution. It may provide
more information about the painting's entry into the collection as a gift.
It reads: "A Peece of three Swittz little/ Entire figures, being an Auntient
[ensign],/ A drummer, and a ffluter done/ by old Peter Brewgill given
by/ M[r] Endimion Porter, in blacke/ and white."[85] As in the Dutch inventories,
grisaille is simply "black and white" painting here. And, with the term *Swittz*,
the soldiers are correctly labeled as mercenaries yet incorrectly designated as
Swiss rather than German.[86] By this time, the flamboyant costume had lost
much of its specificity for viewers. Endymion Porter (1587–1649), a Spanish-
raised English courtier, diplomat, and connoisseur, was instrumental to
the formation of Charles's collection and may have given the small Bruegel
grisaille to Charles. While he might have gifted it before 1625, the *CP* mark

Fig. 31
Anthony van Dyck
Equestrian Portrait of Charles I,
ca. 1638–39
Oil on canvas
144 ½ × 115 in. (367 × 292.1 cm)
National Gallery, London;
Bought, 1885

rules out the possibility that Porter acquired the painting during a 1634–35 diplomatic trip to the Southern Netherlands.[87]

As assiduously recorded by Van der Doort, *The Three Soldiers* hung in the Chair Room at Whitehall Palace, the king's primary residence. There it was in conversation with other relatively small-scale paintings—especially portraits—by sixteenth-century northern European artists such as Dürer, the Antwerp painter Joos van Cleve (ca. 1485–ca. 1540), and Hans Holbein (1497/98–1543), who had worked for the English court during the reign of Henry VIII (1491–1547). Also interspersed were Italian Renaissance works and smaller-scale "modern" pieces such as an oil sketch for the monumental equestrian portrait of Charles I by the seventeenth-century Antwerp painter Anthony van Dyck (1599–1641) (fig. 31).[88]

Charles's vast art collection was particularly strong in Italian Renaissance and Baroque art and in contemporary Flemish paintings by Van Dyck and Peter Paul Rubens (1577–1640), both of whom served the English court at various times.[89] The extent to which Charles I took an interest in his Northern Renaissance paintings, many of which came into his collection en masse as part of larger acquisitions, has been a subject of debate. What is clear is that he preferred portraits and showed less interest in genre subjects. Certainly, *The Three Soldiers* is a far cry from the Italian High Renaissance and Baroque paintings by Titian (1488–1576) or the Carracci—monumental in scale and saturated in color—that the king most favored.[90]

Charles I was not as adept a ruler as he was an art collector. The English Civil War broke out in 1642, following years of conflict over the extent of the power of Parliament versus that of the monarch. In 1649, the king was executed, the monarchy abolished, and Charles I's art collection of around two thousand paintings and sculptures sold under the newly formed Commonwealth.[91] In February 1653, *The Three Soldiers* was sold to Thomas Greene, a merchant-tailor and creditor of the royal family, for just 5 pounds.[92] (The most expensive painting in the sale, by Raphael (1483–1520), cost 2,000 pounds.[93]) Once again, Bruegel's small grisaille was caught up in the vagaries of war.

The history of *The Three Soldiers* in the English royal collection does not end there, however. It reentered the royal collection in 1660 after the restoration of the monarchy under Charles I's son, Charles II (1630–1685), who spent part of his exile in the Dutch Republic and appears to have taken a liking to

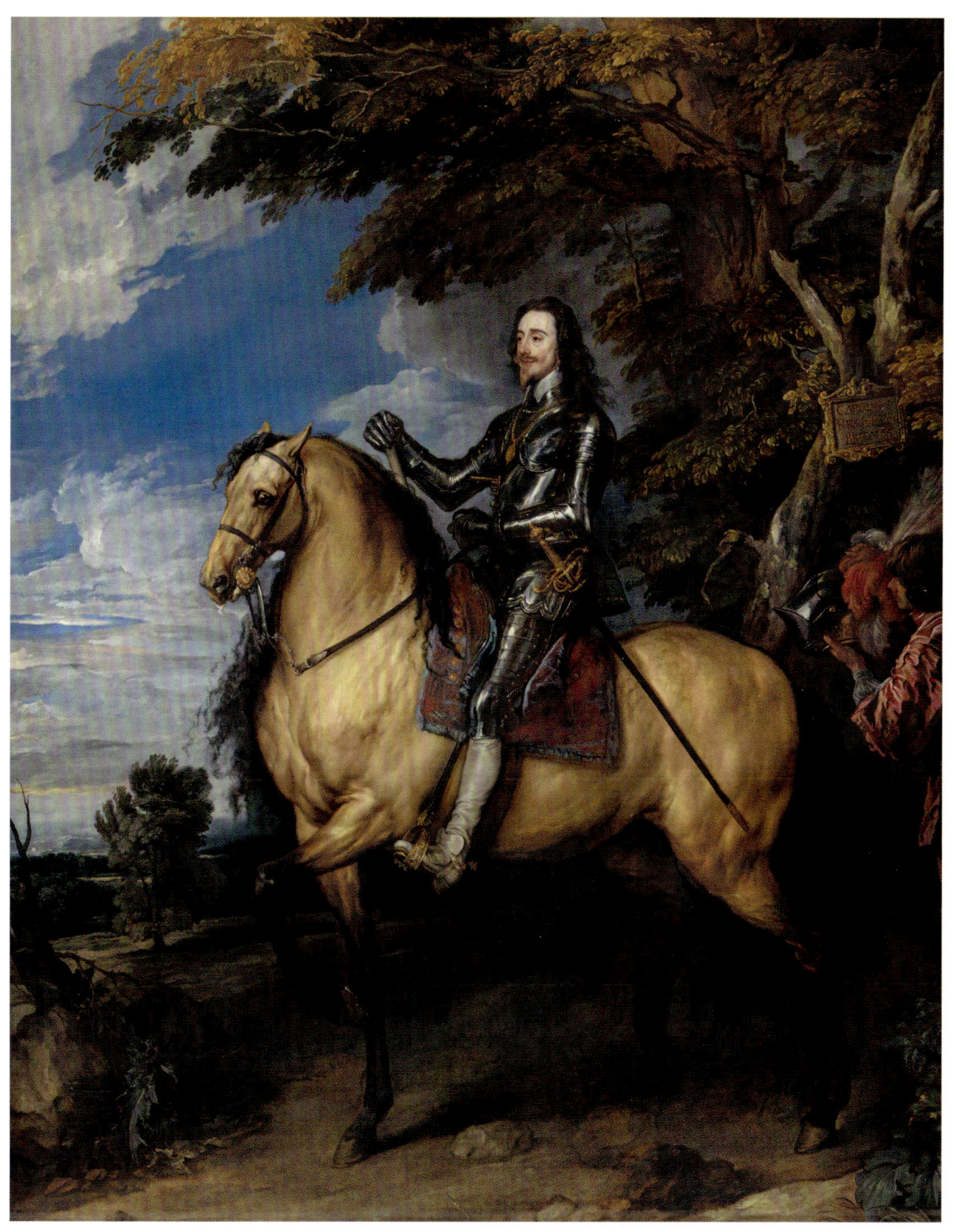

Netherlandish paintings. He acquired the *Massacre of the Innocents* by Pieter Bruegel the Elder (supplementing the copy by Pieter Brueghel the Younger acquired by his father), which hung in the Privy Gallery at Whitehall (see fig. 24).[94] *The Three Soldiers*, however, was relegated to storage, and there is no evidence that it ever went back on view. Changes in taste already begun in the time of Charles I precipitated a decline in appreciation for Bruegel that lasted for centuries. In 1714, at the time of the death of Queen Anne (1665–1714), *The Three Soldiers* was recorded for the last time in the royal collection, in a storeroom at Kensington Palace.[95] At some point soon thereafter, it left royal ownership. In 1722, it was sold in the estate sale of William van Huls (ca. 1649–1722), who had been private secretary under Anne's predecessor, William III (1650–1702). A distinguished collector of early modern northern European artists such as Rembrandt (1606–1669), Van Huls presumably appreciated Bruegel's grisaille more than had recent sovereigns.[96]

After this 1722 sale, the trail of *The Three Soldiers* grows cold until the twentieth century. Remarkably, when the painting resurfaced in the early 1960s, it was at a country sale in the English village of Wingham in Kent, where it was purchased by a Ramsgate dealer named Marks. It sold for only 50 pounds (about 140 dollars at the time); Bruegel's authorship had been completely forgotten. Marks reported that it had been owned by the family from whom he purchased it for about fifty years. However, the family had no concrete evidence pertaining to its whereabouts before that time.[97] Christie's then purchased the painting, recognizing it as an autograph work by Bruegel. It was certainly a good investment—the painting was then purchased in 1964 by the London-based dealer Geoffrey Agnew (1908–1986) and two other dealers for 24,150 pounds (about 67,620 dollars at the time).[98] This price increase, following the correct reattribution, attests to the rise in Bruegel's critical fortunes since their eighteenth-century nadir.

The history of *The Three Soldiers* in Charles I's illustrious collection surely added to the acquisition's appeal for the Frick, but it also complicated the purchase. As Agnew informed then Frick Director Harry D. M. Grier (1914–1972) in August 1965, "the picture is a very important one and has great historical connections within this country." Agnew was obligated to approach the National Gallery in London for first refusal before an export license could be granted to send the painting from England to the United States. Agnew warned Grier that the National Gallery was "very impressed" by the picture and might "exercise their right not to issue an export permit, but to buy it themselves."[99] In a report written in preparation for the proposed acquisition, Frick Curator Edgar Munhall (1933–2016) marveled at the painting's "mysterious" beauty and detailed its history in the collection of Charles I.[100] The Frick was able to obtain a temporary export license for the Acquisitions Committee to consider the work on September 28, with the stipulation that it had to be returned to London before the National Gallery's trustees meeting on October 7.[101]

Writing again to Grier in September, Agnew devised the following strategy:

> After your meeting I would advise that you make no commitment, except privately to tell me how the Trustees feel about its acquisition. I can then, if you wish it, before the National Gallery meeting apply for an on approval licence (which will still not commit you). . . . by applying for an on approval licence instead of a firm sale licence, [you will] not arouse too much the N.G.'s desire to stop the licence! It is a question, you will see, of psychology![102]

Luckily for the Frick, the National Gallery declined to exercise its right to stop the export license. This was likely due simply to a lack of funds at the time rather than shrewd psychological maneuvering on the part of Agnew. The Frick's trustees approved the acquisition, and the painting arrived in New York in mid-October. On January 13, 1966, it was installed in the North Hall.[103] Along with the *Harvesters* (Metropolitan Museum of Art) and the *Wedding Dance* (Detroit Institute of Arts), *The Three Soldiers* remains one of only three autograph works by Bruegel in public collections in the United States.

With today's renewed enthusiasm for Bruegel, the artist's humor is once again abundantly appreciated. Yet Bruegel simultaneously serves as a touchstone for our own era's grappling with societal upheaval.[104] The most famous modern creative response to Bruegel—W. H. Auden's 1938 poem "Musée des Beaux Arts"—was written on the eve of World War II. In Bruegel's panoramic landscapes now hanging in Brussels, Auden saw a commentary on collective indifference to individual suffering. *The Three Soldiers* offers only a tiny sliver of Bruegel's typical panoramic view. Yet, in addressing the puzzle of how the delicate painting relates to the larger context of the onset of the Dutch Revolt in 1568, there is an echo, in the three figures' harmonious circling of one another in an empty space and their resonances with a visual tradition of soldiers off-duty, of the type of figure who, in Auden's phrase, "turns away/

Quite leisurely from the disaster. . . ."[105] Here, however, the stylish mercenaries are implicated in the disaster at hand.

When *The Three Soldiers* is encountered at the Frick, this refined but lesser-known masterpiece demands attention, sparking contemplation and conversation. Examination of the painting in the context of the larger genre of *Landsknechte* within Northern Renaissance art and in the context of 1568 enriches the sense that it responds in an oblique yet sophisticated manner to unfolding historical events, as well as to a diverse array of artistic models. *The Three Soldiers* keeps artistic exploration at the forefront. In this elegiac yet playful composition, Bruegel forged a space of retreat into creativity, elegance, and erudition in a disordered time.

Notes

1 There are traces of the *L* in the gap between *D* and *XVIII*. Despite abrasion in this area, scholars agree that this is the original date. For condition assessments, see Suhr 1965; Scully 2015, 4 [unpaginated].

2 In the Monogrammist's Berlin brothel scene (Gemäldegalerie), prints from the Nuremberg woodcut series (see fig. 3) decorate the brothel. For the Monogrammist, see Ubl 2014.

3 Important recent studies (in descending order) are Silver forthcoming; Burnstock and Serres 2019; Vienna 2018, 285–89, no. 86; London 2018, 239, no. 42; Meganck 2017, 163; Porras 2016, 132–34; Serres 2016; London 2016, 46–51, no. 8; Rotterdam 2015, 268, no. 69; Van der Coelen and Lammertse 2015, 228–30; Silver 2011, 385–86; Sellink 2007, 260–61, no. 170. Additional citations (in ascending order) are Millar 1958–60, 69, 225; Munhall 1966a; Arpino and Bianconi 1967, 113, no. 82; Frick Collection 1968, 142–46; Millar 1970–72, 259; Friedländer 1976, 47, pl. 59; Gibson 1977, 134; Millar 1977, 36, 39; Chastel 1983, 264n.78; Campbell 1985, xxxv, xl, xlii, xliv, 13; Barclay 2010b, no. 144; Jonckheere 2012, 286n.421; The Hague 2015, 58–59, no. 5; Müller and Schauerte 2018, 156–59, 163, 300, 452; Spronk 2018, 359; D. Ekserdjian in London 2018, 87; Kaminska 2019, 187n.1; Ferris 2020, 155, 170–72.

4 Grossmann 1952, 221–22; Serres 2016, 9.

5 Scully 2015. The most comprehensive comparative study of technical findings is Burnstock and Serres 2019, 85–89.

6 Scully 2015, 2. Traces of red earth pigments and azurite are recorded in *Christ and the Woman Taken in Adultery*; Burnstock and Serres 2019, 87.

7 Suhr 1965, 1; Scully 2015, 4; Burnstock and Serres 2019, 87–88.

8 As observed by Sophie Scully. Scully 2015, 3; Burnstock and Serres 2019, 88.

9 My thanks to Sophie Scully for pointing this out.

10 Note that there is abrasion in the standard-bearer.

11 Grossmann 1952, 223–24.

12 Grossmann 1952, 223; Borchert 2009, 239, 252n.2.

13 See Van Eyck's 1435–40 *Annunciation Diptych* (Museo Thyssen-Bornemisza, Madrid). Preimesberger (2011, 48–51) interprets the black marble as touchstone.

14 Most recently, Bol 2023.

15 Smith 1957–59.

16 In relation to Van Eyck, see Preimesberger 2011, 30, 45.

17 Porras 2016, 132.

18 In Italy, the debate was codified by Benedetto Varchi's 1550 questionnaire and by the Florentine Accademia del Disegno (founded 1563); Mendelsohn 1982.

19 Philippot 1966.

20 For Bruegel's Italy trip, see Büttner 2000. On the influence of Clovio, see Grossmann 1973, 16, 25; Serres 2016, 11–12. For grisaille painting and manuscript illumination, see Madrid 2009.

21 As argued by Emma Capron (2020). Capron analyzes preparatory drawings at the J. Paul Getty Museum in Los Angeles, by the Master of the Berlin Roundels, and at the Kupferstichkabinett in Berlin by Jan Swart van Groningen.

22 Hathaway 2016.

23 New York and London 2010; Ainsworth 2014.

24 Ainsworth 2014, 13–16.

25 New York 2014, 98–104, no. 22.

26 Wouk 2018, 467–501, with previous literature.

27 Porras 2016, 133; Serres 2016, 10; Vienna 2018, 288–89. Studies of Bruegel's emulation of Bosch include Ilsink 2009.

28 Porras 2016, 130–42.

29 For the condition and debate regarding technique, see Van der Coelen 2012. There is a print after the *Resurrection* by Philips Galle. However, Bruegel's drawing was not a design for it; Grossmann 1954, 54–63. Also discussed in relationship to grisaille in Grossmann 1952, 221–22; Serres 2016, 14–15. Another autonomous drawing with ink washes, the *Calumny of Apelles* (British Museum, London), is sometimes compared to the grisaille paintings; White 1959, 341; Porras 2016, 115–51.

30 For the Balten collaboration, see Serres 2016, 11. For the Leiden inventory, see Hoogewerff and Van Regteren Altena 1928, 78.

31 On the possibility of a lost original, see Silver 2011, 182–83; Serres 2016, 14. On the Paris version (Fondation Custodia), see London 2016, 52–53, no. 9. The second is in Antwerp (KMSKA).

32 Recent scholarship has debated the extent to which Bruegel was sympathetic to these subjects, especially peasants, beginning with articles by Svetlana Alpers and Hessel Miedema in the 1970s.

33 London 2016, 36–37, nos. 3, 5, 7. Five painted early modern copies of the *Death of the Virgin* survive; London 2016, 26. The dearth of copies of *The Three Soldiers* does indicate diverging reception histories after Bruegel's death but not during his lifetime.

34 Interpretations in line with mine include Meganck 2017, 163. For Bruegel and humanism, see Meadow 2002. Alternate readings of Bruegel and humanism include Müller 1999.

35 Abrah. Ortelius,/ sibi & amicis,/ fieri curabat. Translation from New York and Rotterdam 2001, 258.

36 "Elc van hen, acht ic, hevet noyt bat geconnen./ Zo heeft hun vrients Abrams jonste/ geprickelt hun luyder conste. . . ." Translation from New York and Rotterdam 2001, 258 (original text at 261).

37 New York and Rotterdam 2001, 258.

38 For the painting's and print's reception see, especially, Melion 1996; Meganck 2017, 163–71. Kaminska 2019 (187–211) is the most recent study.

39 For the concept of visual *contrapposti*, see Summers 1972; Summers 1977.

40 In his 1565 *Den hof en boomgaerd der poësien* (LXVI: "Invective, an eenen Quidam schilder. . . ."); De Heere 1969, 80–82, with quote at 81. The unnamed painter attacked in the "Invective" has been identified as Bruegel since Freedberg 1989.

41 Meganck 2017, 158. See also Buchanan 1982; Büttner 1998.

42 For mercenary soldiers in Northern Renaissance art, see Andersson 1978; Moxey 1989, 67–100; Hale 1990; Rogg 2000; Silver 2009; Van der Coelen 2015, 118–22; Bern 2016.

43 Sachs 2016, 162.

44 Moxey 1989, 69–80.

45 For satirical depictions and class, see Moxey 1989, 89–93. For both prints, see Andersson 1998, 188–91. For Sachs's text and Schön's woodcut, see Sachs 2016, 176–77. Note that the shoemaker is a "shoemaker journeyman," i.e., an unmarried man training in his trade. His sweetheart, Ursula, speaks too. She will join the army as a *Dirne* (consort or sex worker). See also Andersson 2018. For disease, see Silver 2006.

46 Erasmus 1997, 329–30 (for the full dialogue, 328–43). Mentioned in Van der Coelen 2015, 118.

47 Erasmus 1997, 334.

48 "Een Tafel spel van een Lansknecht die teghen zijn eyghen schaduwe vocht" (A Chamber Play of a Mercenary who Fought against His Own Shadow); Pikhaus 1988, 1: 63, nos. 91a–c (with audience participation discussed on page 145). The chamber play (literally a "table play") is defined by a small cast and intimate performance setting.

49 There are German examples of Pyramus as a mercenary, including by Graf. Andersson 1978, 57; Silver 2006, 470. For the relationship to a popular "amorous" Dutch play from around 1515, see Veldman 2011, 52. For a discussion of the double entendres in the *Prodigal Son* and *Pyramus and Thisbe*, see Rothstein 2015.

50 Van der Coelen and Lammertse 2015, 230. Compare also the sexual innuendo of the *klotendolk* (ball dagger) discussed in Rotterdam 2015, 154–55.

51 Soergel 2008; Rublack 2010, 110–11, 140–43.

52 Rublack 2010, 60.

53 Rublack 2010, 60, 140–43.

54 Rubin 2018.

55 Rubin 2018, 36.

56 Boone 1996; Roelens 2017a; Roelens 2017b; Roelens 2017c. For Germany and Switzerland, see Puff 2003.

57 Conway 1889, 55. For a different translation, see Ashcroft 2017, 159 and 161n.10, with acknowledgment of sexual innuendo. For the original German, see Dürer 1956, 55. Interpreted in this light in Hale 1990, 37. For homosociality and same-sex desire in Dürer's writings and art, see Schleif 2010; Cavallo 2016. For Dürer's letters, see Brisman 2016, esp. 179.

58 Puff 2003, 43–44, 115–18.

59 "Hoereerders en Buggers"; Leendertz 1924, 218. Discussed in Roelens 2019, 1136. For German mercenaries in the Habsburg army, see Parker 2004, 231–32.

60 For "sodomy" as a catch-all term, see Pleij 2020, 99, 106.

61 A classic text on homosociality is Sedgwick 1985.

62 The *Massacre* was later partially overpainted as a "village plundering." A few *Landsknechte* with slashed or striped hose can nevertheless be found in the painting. See also range of dress (mercenary, Spanish, and Dutch) in a propaganda print of around 1567 in Philadelphia 1993, 46–47, no. 5, and Dutch uniform discussed in Silver 2009, 26.

63 My account is indebted to Arnade 2008. See also Israel 1995; Parker 2002; Duke 2003.

64 Moxey 1977; Freedberg 1988; Jonckheere 2012.

65 Arnade 2008, 1, 6.

66 Marnef 1996.

67 Arnade 2008, 181–91.

68 One source for scholarly arguments comes from Karel van Mander's 1604 biography of the artist, which states that Bruegel had controversial drawings (of unidentified subjects) burned on his deathbed to avoid implications for his wife; Van Mander 1994, 193–94 (fols. 233v–234r).

69 Koerner 2016, 363.

70 Political hubris readings include Carroll 2008, 75–87. For the iconoclasm thesis, see Jonckheere 2014. For an example of a completely different interpretation, see Woodall 2011.

71 Jonckheere 2012, 204–15.

72 Silver 2011, 385; Silver forthcoming.

73 Silver forthcoming.

74 Van der Coelen and Lammertse 2015, 230; Vienna 2018, 287.

75 Van der Coelen and Lammertse 2015, 230.

76 Quoted in Grossmann 1952, 226; Silver forthcoming.

77 Wouk 2018, 344–52 (345 for translation). For translation of "all knowledge," see Filipczak 1987, 13.

78 Healy 2000, 85–90; Wouk 2018, 348–52.

79 For the theme of peace, see Vandommele 2011, esp. 53–133. For the original texts, see Ryckaert 2011. For Bruegel and the rhetoricians (*rederijkers*), see Gibson 1981; Ramakers 1996.

80 Vandommele 2011, 83, 366.

81 "Sterck is den vrede/ als een dryvoudich zeel"; Ryckaert 2011, 1: 748–50. Discussed in Vandommele 2011, 88–91.

82 Vandommele 2011, 91–102. Harmony is further celebrated, for example, in a poetic pageant by the Mechelen chamber De Peoenbloeme depicting Orpheus entrancing animals with music; Ryckaert 2011, 2: 888–90. For the impact of Floris's style on the *landjuweel* (and vice versa), see Vandommele 2011 and Wouk 2018.

83 Millar 1958–60, xiv; Frick Collection 1968, 142; London 2018, 239, no. 42.

84 Millar 1958–60, 69. Manuscript preserved in the British Library (Add. MS. 10112, f. 13).

85 Millar 1958–60, 225. Manuscript preserved in the Victoria and Albert Museum (MS. 86. J. 13, f. 89).

86 London 2016, 51.

87 London 2018, 239, contra London 2016, 51.

88 For the Chair Room inventory, see Millar 1958–60, 62–75; Rumberg and Shawe-Taylor 2018, 20–22.

89 Van Dyck also painted a double portrait of himself with Endymion Porter (Museo del Prado, Madrid). For Van Dyck's impact on English portraiture, see Eaker 2022.

90 Campbell 1985, xxxvi, xxxix; D. Ekserdjian in London 2018, 82–87; D. Ekserdjian in London 2018, 100–105.

91 Royal Collection Trust 2023.

92 Millar 1970–72, 259 (with mention of Greene as merchant-taylor and creditor in Index). For the 1653 dating, see London 2018, 239.

93 Rumberg and Shawe-Taylor 2018, 24.

94 Campbell 1985, xl–xliii, 13–18, no. 9. For the Pieter Brueghel the Younger copy, see Campbell 1985, xxxvii–xxxviii, 19–20, no. 10.

95 For the painting's fate from James II to Queen Anne, see Campbell 1985, xlii–xliv. It is listed in an inventory compiled under James II "in the Kings Great Clossett" possibly at Whitehall; Barclay 2010a; Barclay 2010b, no. 144.

96 Campbell 1985, xliv; London 2016, 51. Van Huls owned a 1669 *Self-Portrait* by Rembrandt (National Gallery, London).

97 Agnew 1966.

98 Christie's 1963–64, 15. Purchased by Agnew, Edward Speelman, and one other dealer.

99 Agnew 1965a.

100 Munhall 1965.

101 Grier 1965.

102 Agnew 1965b.

103 Munhall 1966b.

104 Gibson 2006 is an excellent study of Bruegel and humor. For Bruegel and emerging capitalism and "human nature," see Kavaler 1999 and Honig 2019, respectively.

105 Auden 2023. For Auden and Bruegel, see Nemerov 2005.

BIBLIOGRAPHY

Agnew 1965a Geoffrey Agnew. Personal communication with Harry D. M. Grier, August 31, 1965. The Frick Collection - Central Files, 1966 - Acquisitions - Bruegel, "Three Soldiers," 1965–66. The Frick Collection/Frick Art Reference Library Archives.

Agnew 1965b Geoffrey Agnew. Personal communication with Harry D. M. Grier, September 12, 1965. The Frick Collection - Central Files, 1966 - Acquisitions - Bruegel, "Three Soldiers," 1965–66. The Frick Collection/Frick Art Reference Library Archives.

Agnew 1966 Julian Agnew. Personal communication with Harry D. M. Grier, January 11, 1966. The Frick Collection - Central Files, 1966 - Acquisitions - Bruegel, "Three Soldiers," 1965–66. The Frick Collection/Frick Art Reference Library Archives.

Ainsworth 2014 Ainsworth, Maryan W. *Jan Gossart's Trip to Rome and His Route to Paragone*. The Hague, 2014.

Andersson 1978 Andersson, Christiane. *Dirnen, Krieger, Narren: Ausgewählte Zeichnungen von Urs Graf*. Basel, 1978.

Andersson 1998 Andersson, Christiane. "Von 'Metzen' und 'Dirnen': Frauenbilder in Kriegsdarstellungen der Frühen Neuzeit." In *Landsknechte, Soldatenfrauen und Nationalkrieger: Militär, Krieg und Geschlechterordnung im historischen Wandel*, edited by Karen Hagemann and Ralf Pröve, 171–98. Frankfurt and New York, 1998.

Andersson 2018 Andersson, Christiane. "Harlots and Camp Followers: Swiss Renaissance Drawings of Young Women circa 1520." In *The Youth of Early Modern Women*, edited by Elizabeth S. Cohen and Margaret Reeves, 117–34. Amsterdam, 2018.

Arnade 2008 Arnade, Peter. *Beggars, Iconoclasts, and Civic Patriots: The Political Culture of the Dutch Revolt*. Ithaca, NY, 2008.

Arpino and Bianconi 1967 Arpino, Giovanni, and Piero Bianconi. *L'opera completa di Bruegel*. Milan, 1967.

Ashcroft 2017 Ashcroft, Jeffrey, ed. and trans. *Albrecht Dürer: Documentary Biography: Dürer's Personal and Aesthetic Writings: Words on Pictures, Family, Legal and Business Documents: The Artist in the Writings of Contemporaries*. Vol. 1. New Haven, 2017.

Auden 2023 Auden, W. H. "Musée des Beaux Arts." Poetry Foundation. Accessed September 2023. https://www.poetryfoundation.org/poems/159364/musee-des-beaux-arts-63a1efde036cd.

Barclay 2010a Barclay, Andrew. "The Inventories of the English Royal Collection, *temp.* James II." *Journal of the History of Collections* 22, no. 1 (2010): 1–13.

Barclay 2010b Barclay, Andrew. Supplement to "The Inventories of the English Royal Collection, *temp.* James II." *Journal of the History of Collections* 22, no. 1 (2010): 1–13. https://doi.org/10.1093/jhc/fhp031.

Bern 2016 Susan Marti, ed. *Söldner, Bilderstürmer, Totentänzer: Mit Niklaus Manuel durch die Zeit der Reformation*. Exh. cat. Bern (Bernisches Historisches Museum), 2016.

Bol 2023 Bol, Marjolijn. *The Varnish and the Glaze: Painting Splendor with Oil, 1100–1500*. Chicago, 2023.

Boone 1996 Boone, Marc. "State Power and Illicit Sexuality: The Persecution of Sodomy in Late Medieval Bruges." *Journal of Medieval History* 22, no. 2 (1996): 135–53.

Borchert 2009 Borchert, Till-Holger. "*Color Lapidum:* A Survey of Late Medieval Grisaille." In Madrid 2009, 239–53.

Brisman 2016 Brisman, Shira. *Albrecht Dürer and the Epistolary Mode of Address.* Chicago, 2016.

Buchanan 1982 Buchanan, Iain. "Dürer and Abraham Ortelius." *Burlington Magazine* 124, no. 957 (1982): 734–41.

Burnstock and Serres 2019 Burnstock, Aviva, and Karen Serres. "Pieter Bruegel the Elder's Grisaille Paintings." In *Bruegel: The Hand of the Master: Essays in Context,* edited by Alice Hoppe-Harnoncourt, Elke Oberthaler, Sabine Pénot, Manfred Sellink, and Ron Spronk, 82–91. Lichtervelde, 2019.

Büttner 1998 Büttner, Nils. "Abraham Ortelius comme collectionneur." In *Abraham Ortelius (1527–1598): Cartographe et humaniste,* edited by Pierre Cockshaw and Francine de Nave, 169–80. Turnhout, Belgium, 1998.

Büttner 2000 Büttner, Nils. "'Quid Siculas sequeris per mille pericula terras?': Ein Beitrag zur Biographie Pieter Bruegels d. Ä. und zur Kulturgeschichte der niederländischen Italienreise." *Marburger Jahrbuch für Kunstwissenschaft* 27 (2000): 209–42.

Campbell 1985 Campbell, Lorne. *The Early Flemish Pictures in the Collection of Her Majesty the Queen.* Cambridge, England, and New York, 1985.

Capron 2020 Capron, Emma. "Frick Perspectives: Northern Lights." Lecture presented at The Frick Collection, New York, February 22, 2020. Accessed September 2023. https://www.youtube.com/watch?v=2E06u_vxx5Q&t=7s.

Carroll 2008 Carroll, Margaret D. *Painting and Politics in Northern Europe: Van Eyck, Bruegel, Rubens, and Their Contemporaries.* University Park, PA, 2008.

Cavallo 2016 Cavallo, Bradley J. "The Men's Bathhouse of 1496–1497: Problems of Sexual Signification." *Journal for Early Modern Cultural Studies* 16, no. 4 (2016): 9–37.

Chastel 1983 Chastel, André. *The Sack of Rome, 1527.* Translated by Beth Archer. Princeton, NJ, 1983.

Christie's 1963–64 Christie's London. *Review of the Year.* London, 1963–64.

Conway 1889 Conway, William Martin. *Literary Remains of Albrecht Dürer.* Cambridge, England, 1889.

De Heere 1969 De Heere, Lucas. *Den hof en boomgaerd der poësien.* Edited by W. Waterschoot. Zwolle, 1969. Consulted via DBNL. Accessed September 2023. https://www.dbnl.org/tekst/heer001denh01_01/heer001denh01_01_0003.php.

Duke 2003 Duke, Alastair C. *Reformation and Revolt in the Low Countries.* 1st paperback ed. London and New York, 2003.

Dürer 1956 Dürer, Albrecht. *Schriftlicher Nachlass.* Vol. 1. Edited by Hans Rupprich. Berlin, 1956.

Eaker 2022 Eaker, Adam. *Van Dyck and the Making of English Portraiture.* London and New Haven, 2022.

Erasmus 1997 Erasmus, Desiderius. *Collected Works of Erasmus: Colloquies.* Vol. 39. Translated and annotated by Craig R. Thompson. Toronto, Buffalo, and London, 1997.

Ferris 2020 Ferris, Toby. *Short Life in a Strange World: Birth to Death in 42 Panels*. New York, 2020.

Filipczak 1987 Filipczak, Zirka. *Picturing Art in Antwerp, 1550–1700*. Princeton, 1987.

Freedberg 1988 Freedberg, David. "Iconoclasm and Painting in the Revolt of the Netherlands, 1566–1609." PhD diss., Oxford University, 1988 [1972].

Freedberg 1989 Freedberg, David. "Allusion and Topicality in the Work of Pieter Bruegel: The Implications of a Forgotten Polemic." In *The Prints of Pieter Bruegel the Elder*, edited by David Freedberg, 53–65. Exh. cat. Tokyo (Bridgestone Museum of Art), Kurume (Ishibashi Museum of Art), Tsu (Mie Prefectural Art Museum), and Hiroshima (Hiroshima Prefectural Museum of Art), 1989.

Frick Collection 1968 *The Frick Collection: An Illustrated Catalogue*. Vol. 1, *Paintings: American, British, Dutch, Flemish and German*. New York, 1968.

Friedländer 1976 Friedländer, Max J. *Early Netherlandish Painting*. Vol. 14, *Pieter Bruegel*. Translated by Heinz Norden. Leiden, 1976.

Gibson 1977 Gibson, Walter S. *Bruegel*. Amsterdam and Brussels, 1977.

Gibson 1981 Gibson, Walter S. "Artists and *Rederijkers* in the Age of Bruegel." *Art Bulletin* 63, no. 3 (1981): 426–46.

Gibson 2006 Gibson, Walter S. *Pieter Bruegel and the Art of Laughter*. Berkeley, CA, 2006.

Grier 1965 Grier, Harry D. M. Personal communication with Evelyn Joll, September 8, 1965. The Frick Collection - Central Files, 1966 - Acquisitions - Bruegel, "Three Soldiers," 1965–66. The Frick Collection/Frick Art Reference Library Archives.

Grossmann 1952 Grossmann, Fritz. "Bruegel's 'Woman Taken in Adultery' and Other Grisailles." *Burlington Magazine* 94, no. 593 (1952): 218–27.

Grossmann 1954 Grossmann, Fritz. "The Drawings of Pieter Bruegel the Elder in the Museum Boymans and Some Problems of Attribution." *Bulletin Museum Boymans Rotterdam* 5, no. 2 (1954): 41–63.

Grossmann 1973 Grossmann, Fritz. *Pieter Bruegel: Complete Edition of the Paintings*. 3rd ed. London and New York, 1973.

Hale 1990 Hale, J. R. *Artists and Warfare in the Renaissance*. London and New Haven, 1990.

Hathaway 2016 Hathaway, Nenagh. "Jheronimus Bosch and the Netherlandish Grisaille." In *Jheronimus Bosch: His Life and His Work*, edited by Ron Spronk, Eric de Bruyn, Matthijs Ilsink, Jos Koldeweij, and Hannah Gooiker, 106–22. 's-Hertogenbosch, The Netherlands, 2016.

Healy 2000 Healy, Fiona. "Bedrooms and Banquets: Mythology in Sixteenth-Century Flemish Painting." In *Concept, Design, and Execution in Flemish Painting (1550–1700)*, edited by Arnout Balis, Carl Van de Velde, and Hans Vlieghe, 73–96. Turnhout, Belgium, 2000.

Honig 2019 Honig, Elizabeth. *Pieter Bruegel and the Idea of Human Nature*. London, 2019.

Hoogewerff and Van Regteren Altena 1928 Hoogewerff, G. J., and J. Q. van Regteren Altena, eds. *Arnoldus Buchelius, "Res pictoriae": Aanteekeningen over kunstenaars en kunstwerken, 1583–1639.* The Hague, 1928.

Ilsink 2009 Ilsink, Matthijs. *Bosch en Bruegel als Bosch: Kunst over kunst bij Pieter Bruegel (c. 1528–1569) en Jheronimus Bosch (c. 1450–1516).* Nijmegen, 2009.

Israel 1995 Israel, Jonathan. *The Dutch Republic: Its Rise, Greatness, and Fall, 1477–1806.* Oxford, 1995.

Jonckheere 2012 Jonckheere, Koenraad. *Antwerp Art after Iconoclasm: Experiments in Decorum, 1566–1585.* Translated by Katy Kist and Jennifer Kilian, with Paul van Calster. Brussels, 2012.

Jonckheere 2014 Jonckheere, Koenraad. "An Allegory of Artistic Choice in Times of Trouble: Pieter Bruegel's *Tower of Babel.*" *Nederlands Kunsthistorisch Jaarboek* 64 (2014): 186–213.

Kaminska 2019 Kaminska, Barbara A. *Pieter Bruegel the Elder: Religious Art for the Urban Community.* Leiden and Boston, 2019.

Kavaler 1999 Kavaler, Ethan Matt. *Pieter Bruegel: Parables of Order and Enterprise.* Cambridge, England, and New York, 1999.

Koerner 2016 Koerner, Joseph. *Bosch and Bruegel: From Enemy Painting to Everyday Life.* Princeton, NJ, and Washington, DC, 2016.

Leendertz 1924 Leendertz, P., Jr. *Het geuzenliedboek: Naar de oude drukken uit de nalatenschap van Dr. E. T. Kuiper.* Vol. 1. Zutphen, The Netherlands, 1924.

London 2016 Karen Serres, ed. *Bruegel in Black and White: Three Grisailles Reunited.* Exh cat. London (Courtauld Gallery), 2016.

London 2018 Per Rumberg and Desmond Shawe-Taylor, eds. *Charles I: King and Collector.* Exh. cat. London (Royal Academy of Arts), 2018.

Madrid 2009 Till-Holger Borchert, ed. *Jan van Eyck: Grisallas.* Exh. cat. Madrid (Museo Thyssen-Bornemisza), 2009.

Marnef 1996 Marnef, Guido. *Antwerp in the Age of Reformation: Underground Protestantism in a Commercial Metropolis, 1550–1577.* Translated by J. C. Grayson. Baltimore, 1996.

Meadow 2002 Meadow, Mark. *Pieter Bruegel the Elder's Netherlandish Proverbs and the Practice of Rhetoric.* Zwolle, The Netherlands, 2002.

Meganck 2017 Meganck, Tine. *Erudite Eyes: Friendship, Art and Erudition in the Network of Abraham Ortelius (1527–1598).* Leiden and Boston, 2017.

Melion 1996 Melion, Walter S. "'*Ego enim quasi obdormivi*': Salvation and Blessed Sleep in Philip Galle's *Death of the Virgin* after Pieter Bruegel." *Nederlands Kunsthistorisch Jaarboek* 47 (1996): 14–53.

Mendelsohn 1982 Mendelsohn, Leatrice. *Paragoni: Benedetto Varchi's "Due lezzioni" and Cinquecento Art Theory.* Ann Arbor, MI, 1982.

Millar 1958–60 Millar, Oliver. "Abraham van der Doort's Catalogue of the Collections of Charles I." *Volume of the Walpole Society* 37 (1958–60): xiii–243.

Millar 1970–72 Millar, Oliver. "The Inventories and Valuations of the King's Goods 1649–1651." *Volume of the Walpole Society* 43 (1970–72): xi–443.

Millar 1977 Millar, Oliver. *The Queen's Pictures*. New York, 1977.

Moxey 1977 Moxey, Keith. "Aertsen, Beuckelaer, and Secular Painting in the Reformation." PhD diss., University of Chicago, 1977 [1974].

Moxey 1989 Moxey, Keith. *Peasants, Warriors, and Wives*. Chicago, 1989.

Müller 1999 Müller, Jürgen. *Das Paradox als Bildform: Studien zur Ikonologie Pieter Bruegels d.Ä.* Munich, 1999.

Müller and Schauerte 2018 Müller, Jürgen, and Thomas Schauerte. *Pieter Bruegel: The Complete Works*. Translated by Abigail Prohaska. Cologne, 2018.

Munhall 1965 Munhall, Edgar. The Frick Collection, Curatorial Report, August 1965. Unpublished internal document.

Munhall 1966a Munhall, Edgar. "The Frick's Brueghel." *Apollo* 83, no. 51 (1966): 393.

Munhall 1966b Munhall, Edgar. The Frick Collection, memo to guards and sales information staff, January 13, 1966. Unpublished internal document.

Nemerov 2005 Nemerov, Alexander. "The Flight of Form: Auden, Bruegel, and the Turn to Abstraction in the 1940s." *Critical Inquiry* 31, no. 4 (2005): 780–810.

New York 2014 Elizabeth Cleland, ed. *Grand Design: Pieter Coecke van Aelst and Renaissance Tapestry*. Exh. cat. New York (Metropolitan Museum of Art), 2014.

New York and London 2010 Maryan W. Ainsworth, ed. *Man, Myth, and Sensual Pleasures: Jan Gossart's Renaissance: The Complete Works*. Exh. cat. New York (Metropolitan Museum of Art) and London (National Gallery), 2010.

New York and Rotterdam 2001 Nadine Orenstein, ed. *Pieter Bruegel the Elder: Drawings and Prints*. Exh. cat. New York (Metropolitan Museum of Art) and Rotterdam (Museum Boijmans Van Beuningen), 2001.

Parker 2002 Parker, Geoffrey. *The Dutch Revolt*. London, 2002.

Parker 2004 Parker, Geoffrey. *The Army of Flanders and the Spanish Road, 1567–1659: The Logistics of Spanish Victory and Defeat in the Low Countries' Wars*. Cambridge, England, and New York, 2004.

Philadelphia 1993 James Tanis and Daniel Horst. *Images of Discord: A Graphic Interpretation of the Opening Decades of the Eighty Years' War / De tweedracht verbeeld: Prentkunst als propaganda aan het begin van de Tachtigjarige Oorlog*. Exh. cat. Philadelphia (Philadelphia Museum of Art), 1993.

Philippot 1966 Philippot, Paul. "Les grisailles et les 'degrés de réalité' de l'image dans la peinture flamande des XVe et XVIe siècles." *Bulletin Musées Royaux des Beaux-Arts de Belgique* 15 (1966): 225–46.

Pikhaus 1988 Pikhaus, Patricia. *Het tafelspel bij de rederijkers.* 2 vols. Ghent, 1988.

Pleij 2020 Pleij, Herman. *Oefeningen in genot: Liefde en lust in de late Middeleeuwen.* Amsterdam, 2020.

Porras 2016 Porras, Stephanie. *Pieter Bruegel's Historical Imagination.* University Park, PA, 2016.

Preimesberger 2011 Preimesberger, Rudolf. *Paragons and Paragone: Van Eyck, Raphael, Michelangelo, Caravaggio, and Bernini.* Translated by Sabine Eiche and Fiona Elliott. Los Angeles, 2011.

Puff 2003 Puff, Helmut. *Sodomy in Reformation Germany and Switzerland, 1400–1600.* Chicago, 2003.

Ramakers 1996 Ramakers, Bart. "Bruegel en de rederijkers: Schilderkunst en literatuur in de zestiende eeuw." *Nederlands Kunsthistorisch Jaarboek* 47 (1996): 80–105.

Roelens 2017a Roelens, Jonas. "Gossip, Defamation, and Sodomy in the Early Modern Southern Netherlands." *Renaissance Studies* 32, no. 2 (2017): 236–52.

Roelens 2017b Roelens, Jonas. "Fornicating Foreigners: Sodomy, Migration, and Urban Society in the Southern Low Countries (1400–1700)." *Dutch Crossing* 42, no. 3 (2017): 229–46.

Roelens 2017c Roelens, Jonas. "Middeleeuwse brandstapels." In *Verzwegen verlangen: Een geschiedenis van homoseksualiteit in België*, by Wannes Dupont, Elwin Hofman, and Jonas Roelens, 23–55. Antwerp, 2017.

Roelens 2019 Roelens, Jonas. "Songs of Sodom: Singing about the Unmentionable Vice in the Early Modern Low Countries." *Journal of Homosexuality* 66, no. 8 (2019): 1126–47.

Rogg 2000 Rogg, Matthias. *Landsknechte und Reisläufer: Bilder vom Soldaten: Ein Stand in der Kunst des 16. Jahrhunderts.* Paderborn, 2000.

Rothstein 2015 Rothstein, Bret. "Jan van Hemessen's Anatomy of Parody." In *The Anthropomorphic Lens: Anthropomorphism, Microcosm and Analogy in Early Modern Thought and Visual Arts*, edited by Walter S. Melion, Bret Rothstein, and Michel Weemans, 457–79. Leiden, 2015.

Rotterdam 2015 Peter van der Coelen and Friso Lammertse, eds. *De ontdekking van het dagelijks leven: Van Bosch tot Bruegel.* Exh. cat. Rotterdam (Museum Boijmans Van Beuningen), 2015.

Royal Collection Trust 2023 Royal Collection Trust. "Charles I." Accessed September 2023. https://lostcollection.rct.uk/charles-i.

Rubin 2018 Rubin, Patricia. *Seen from Behind: Perspectives on the Male Body and Renaissance Art.* New Haven, 2018.

Rublack 2010 Rublack, Ulinka. *Dressing Up: Cultural Identity in Renaissance Europe.* Oxford, 2010.

Rumberg and Shawe-Taylor 2018 Rumberg, Per, and Desmond Shawe-Taylor. "'The greatest amateur of paintings among the princes of the world.'" In London 2018, 17–25.

Ryckaert 2011 Ryckaert, Ruud, ed. *De Antwerpse spelen van 1561: Naar de editie Silvius (Antwerpen 1562) uitgegeven met inleiding, annotaties en registers.* 2 vols. Ghent, 2011.

Sachs 2016 Sachs, Hans. *Landsknechte bei Hans Sachs: Alte und neue Landsknechtstexte auf Einblattdrucken mit Holzschnitten.* Edited by Hans Blosen and Harald Pors. Berlin, 2016.

Schleif 2010 Schleif, Corine. "Albrecht Dürer between Agnes Frey and Willibald Pirckheimer." In *The Essential Dürer*, edited by Larry Silver and Jeffrey Chipps Smith, 185–205. Philadelphia, 2010.

Scully 2015 Scully, Sophie. The Metropolitan Museum of Art. Examination record of Pieter Bruegel the Elder, *Three Soldiers*, July 2015. Unpublished internal document.

Sedgwick 1985 Sedgwick, Eve Kosofsky. *Between Men: English Literature and Male Homosocial Desire.* New York, 1985.

Sellink 2007 Sellink, Manfred. *Bruegel: The Complete Paintings, Drawings, and Prints.* Ghent, 2007.

Serres 2016 Serres, Karen. "Bruegel's Grisailles." In London 2016, 9–16.

Silver 2006 Silver, Larry. "*Pox vobiscum*: Early Modern German Art and Syphilis." In *Tributes in Honor of James H. Marrow: Studies in Painting and Manuscript Illumination of the Late Middle Ages and Northern Renaissance*, edited by Jeffrey F. Hamburger and Anne S. Korteweg, 465–76. London, 2006.

Silver 2009 Silver, Larry. "The *Landsknecht*: Summer Soldier and Sunshine Patriot." In *The Plains of Mars: European War Prints, 1500–1825*, edited by James Clifton and Leslie Scattone. Exh. cat. Houston (Museum of Fine Arts, Houston), 2009, 16–29.

Silver 2011 Silver, Larry. *Pieter Bruegel.* New York, 2011.

Silver forthcoming Silver, Larry. *Bruegel, Soldiers, and Kings.* Leuven, forthcoming.

Smith 1957–59 Smith, Molly Teasdale. "The Use of Grisaille as a Lenten Observance." *Marsyas* 8 (1957–59): 43–54.

Soergel 2008 Soergel, Philip M. "Baggy Pants and Demons: Andreas Musculus's Condemnation of the Evils of Sixteenth-Century Dress." In *Recht und Verhalten in vormodernen Gesellschaften: Festschrift für Neithard Bulst*, edited by Andrea Bendlage, Andreas Priever, and Peter Schuster, 139–54. Bielefeld, 2008.

Spronk 2018 Spronk, Ron. "On Pieter Bruegel's Creative Process." In Vienna 2018, 355–67.

Suhr 1965 Suhr, William. The Frick Collection. Record of inspection of Pieter Bruegel the Elder, *Three Soldiers*, September 28, 1965. Unpublished internal document.

Summers 1972 Summers, David. "*Maniera* and Movement: The *Figura Serpentinata*." *Art Quarterly* 35, no. 3 (1972): 269–301.

Summers 1977 Summers, David. "*Contrapposto*: Style and Meaning in Renaissance Art." *Art Bulletin* 59, no. 3 (1977): 336–61.

The Hague 2015 Lea van der Vinde, ed. *The Frick Collection: Art Treasures from New York.* Exh. cat. The Hague (Mauritshuis), 2015.

Ubl 2014 Ubl, Matthias. *Der Braunschweiger Monogrammist: Wegbereiter der niederländischen Genremalerei vor Bruegel.* Petersberg, 2014.

Van der Coelen 2012 Van der Coelen, Peter. "Pieter Bruegel the Elder, *The Resurrection of Christ*, c. 1562." In *Netherlandish Drawings of the Fifteenth and Sixteenth Centuries: Artists Born before 1581*, edited by Yvonne Bleyerveld, Albert J. Elen, Judith Niessen, et al. Rotterdam, 2012. Online collections catalogue of the Museum Boijmans Van Beuningen. Accessed September 2023. https://www.boijmans.nl/en/collection/research/netherlandish-drawings-of-the-fifteenth-and-sixteenth-centuries.

Van der Coelen 2015 Van der Coelen, Peter. "Landsknechten, boeren, en bordelen: Nederlandse en Duitse genregrafiek van Sebald Beham tot Jan Vermeyen." In Rotterdam 2015, 117–39.

Van der Coelen and Lammertse 2015 Van der Coelen, Peter, and Friso Lammertse. "Niet zonder te lachen: Pieter Bruegel de Oude." In Rotterdam 2015, 201–33.

Vandommele 2011 Vandommele, Jeroen. *Als in een spiegel: Vrede, kennis en gemeenschap op het Antwerpse Landjuweel van 1561.* Hilversum, 2011.

Van Mander 1994 Van Mander, Karel. *The Lives of the Illustrious Netherlandish and German Painters, from the First Edition of the* Schilder-boeck *(1603–1604): Preceded by the Lineage, Circumstances and Place of Birth, Life and Works of Karel van Mander, Painter and Poet and Likewise his Death and Burial, from the Second Edition of the* Schilder-boeck *(1616–1618).* Vol. 1. Translated by Hessel Miedema. Doornspijk, The Netherlands, 1994.

Veldman 2011 Veldman, Ilja M. "Beeldtraditie en vernieuwing: Onderwerpskeuze in de Leidse kunst van 1480–1550." In *Lucas van Leyden en de Renaissance*, edited by Christiaan Vogelaar, 43–77. Exh. cat. Leiden (Museum De Lakenhal), 2011.

Vienna 2018 Elke Oberthaler, Sabine Pénot, Manfred Sellink, and Ron Spronk, with Alice Hoppe-Harnoncourt. *Bruegel: The Master.* Exh. cat. Vienna (Kunsthistorisches Museum), 2018.

White 1959 White, Christopher. "Pieter Bruegel the Elder: Two New Drawings." *Burlington Magazine* 101, nos. 678–79 (1959): 336–41.

Woodall 2011 Woodall, Joanna. "Lost in Translation? Thinking about Classical and Vernacular Art in Antwerp, 1540–1580." In *Understanding Art in Antwerp: Classicising the Popular, Popularising the Classic (1540–1580)*, edited by Bart Ramakers, 1–24. Louvain, 2011.

Wouk 2018 Wouk, Edward. *Frans Floris (1519/20–70): Imagining a Northern Renaissance.* Leiden and Boston, 2018.

INDEX

Page numbers in *italics* refer to the illustrations.